Antisthenes: The Founder of Cynicism

His Life, His Work, His Doctrine

I0530228

Charles Chappuis

Translated by Richard Robinson

Sunny Lou Publishing Company
Portland, Oregon, USA
http://www.sunnyloupublishing.com

Corrected: 2024 November 13
Original Publication Date: 2024 October 10

ISBN: 978-1-955392-73-0

This translation from French is based on *Antisthène: Thèse Présentée à la Faculté des Lettres de Paris*, by Charles Chappuis, published by Auguste Durand, Libraire, Paris, 1854.

Contents

Translator's Preface

This, Charles Chappuis' brochure, is a little gem. It is with affection that I call it a brochure, in the sense that it is short, but not *too* short, and to the point. It contains just about everything that one might wish to know about Antisthenes, without its being exhaustive, – and without having at our disposal his own works, all of which are, at least the important ones, apparently lost; recent improvements in technology might correct that loss soon though, allowing us to read the burnt scrolls of antiquity from the burnt Library of Alexandria finally, Antisthenes' writings being assuredly among them.

Chappuis' book puts Antisthenes in historical context, both as a historical person and, more importantly, as a philosopher – a man of serious thought and relevance, who will regain we hope his rightful place beside his teacher Socrates; beside Plato, a co-pupil of Socrates and a competitor of ideas, contemporaneously teaching at a different gymnasium than him (Plato at the Academy, Antisthenes at the Cynosarges); beside Diogenes, Antisthenes' pupil and the subsequent head, some say (wrongly) the founder, of Cynicism; beside Crates, Diogenes' pupil, and Crates' pupil Zeno, the founder of Stoicism. And so on and so forth. Not to mention the Eleatics and Sophists and various other Greek philosophers in a long line extending from before Socrates to after Zeno.

Only some of the extensive footnotes from the

original work have been translated and preserved in this English edition. Handpicked are those that were felt to add clarity to the otherwise clear and sufficient statements made in the body of the text.

Scholars of Greek philosophy, then, or scholars in general, who feel the need for the *entirety* of the footnotes, with the references to sources, should recur to the original French text by Charles Chappuis.

Not included in this translation as well, primarily for reasons of laziness, are notes from the appendix of the original: a list of individuals in antiquity who bore the same name of Antisthenes; a chronological discussion of the principal dates in the life of Antisthenes; and a discussion about whether Plato had made an allusion to Antisthenes' ideas on the nature of pleasure, in *Philebus* and in *The Republic*.

All in all, and despite these omissions, we trust that the reader, both casual and serious, will find this small volume by Charles Chappuis, this brochure on Antisthenes' life, works, and philosophical doctrine – delightful, intelligible, and informative. It restores to the founder of Cynicism, if ever he lost it, his proper place in the history of Greek philosophy.

– Richard Robinson, Aleutian Islands, September 13, 2024

Foreword

Antisthenes is one of the most remarkable philosophers among the Socratics: if the beauty of his style and the charm of his works had him compared to Plato or Xenophon, the severity of his principles and the austerity of his life had the ancients comparing him to Socrates. He founded a school that makes great ideas and great aberrations famous; and these same Cynics, whose bizarre behavior we deplore, sometimes manage to surprise us with admiration. Diogenes' excesses and the eccentricities of his successors made their school fall into complete disrepute. But Antisthenes' thought attracted worthier representatives. He is not merely the precursor of Stoicism, he is the original author of that great philosophical movement; and thus, in the Greek and Roman world, he had more influence perhaps than Plato himself.

For these various reasons, Antisthenes draws the attention of philosophers, and he merits being the object of a special study. By consecrating this work to him, we attempt to fill one of the most regrettable gaps in the history of the Greek schools [of philosophy].

In the first part of this study we will present Antisthenes' life and work; in the second, we will provide an exposition and appreciation of his doctrine. We will not follow the Cynic school, which lasted for nearly ten centuries, to the end of its days; but we will include a discussion of the interesting and rich epoch that ended with Antisthenes' immediate disciples and successors, until the beginning of Stoicism.

Part I:
Antisthenes' Life and Works

Chapter 1: Antisthenes' Life

Antisthenes was born in Athens[1] around the year 444 BC. His father was named Antisthenes[2] and was of the same birthplace; but his mother was originally from Thrace.

According to Solon's laws, laws that had fallen into desuetude multiple times, but were always reestablished by Athenian pride, no one was a citizen if his father and his mother were not both freemen and Athenians. Being the son of a foreign mother, Antisthenes belonged, like illegitimate children and freedmen, to the class looked down upon as *νόθοι* [bastards, or illegitimate children].

Thus, placed by birth in the inferior ranks of society and in a condition next to that of slaves, he learned to despise the privileges that fate had refused him; if Athenians boasted of having been born from the sun itself, he responded that "the grasshoppers and snails share that honor with them."[3] When he was reminded that he was not the child of two freemen, he said,"Is an invincible fighter the son of two fighters?" And if someone asked him about the origins of his mother, he retorted, "The mother of the Gods is a

[1]Original footnote: Athens: Plato, *Phædus*, p. 59, b. – Laërt. I, 19; VI, 1. – Suidas, voce Ἀντισθένης.

[2]Original footnote: Laërt., VI, 1. – Suidas, see Ἀντισθένης.

[3]Original footnote: Laërt., VI, 1.

Phrygian."[4]

When he distinguished himself by his valor in a fight that took place under the walls of Tanagra, Socrates said, "Do you think that someone could show so much courage and strength of spirit if he were born of two Athenians?" It was among other νόθοι that Antisthenes' character was formed, that he developed his doctrine and his destiny, and that he learned how to love obscurity, poverty, and hard work.

In his youth he attended lessons by the Sophists and especially those by Gorgias. At the school of that man, who had seduced the Athenians and all of Greece by his brilliant and scholarly eloquence, Antisthenes developed the style that was later admired in his own work, particularly in the dialog on *Truth* and in the *Exhortations*. He strove, by his teacher's example, to expose with equal advantage both the pros and cons [of a position]; and he was supposed to have praised and censured the Isthmic games of the Athenians, Thebans, and Lacedaemonians; but after seeing one of the crowded competitions of athletes from those different cities, he renounced the project. To counter blame with praise, ψέξαι καὶ ἐπαινέσαι, to make oneself admired from the get-go, then to exceed oneself, that is the act of a Sophist; but the young man's timidity gained the upper hand, and one senses a certain honesty in him, a natural rectitude that Gorgias could not completely destroy, and which will later develop into a better teacher.

---

[4]Original footnote: ib., 4.

Antisthenes knew both Prodicus of Ceos and Hippias of Elis; he esteemed their talent and he led pupils to them: "I know," Socrates said to him in Xenophon's *Symposium*, "that it is you who had first brought Callias here, to the wise man Prodicus, seeing that the former was in love with philosophy and the latter was in need of money; I know that you had also introduced him to Hippias of Elis who gave him lessons in artificial memory."[5]

Thus, Antisthenes, the disciple of Gorgias, devoted to Prodicus and Hippias, developed his mind in the commerce of these celebrated Sophists. But did he also give lessons in Sophism according to their example? It is something that one is permitted to doubt, for the testimonies on this subject are not very satisfying, and Antisthenes was still quite young when he separated from Gorgias. Soon he was supposed to have grown to despise those rhetors' exercises, and he started to criticize that school where he had made his first assays.

He did not spend more than four years among the Sophists, and, around the year 423 BC, he became a disciple of Socrates. He became attached to him with admiration, with love; to the former obscurities in his mind succeeded a bright light; regions of philosophy seemed to open up before him and he followed his new guide with that zeal, with that joy, which the love of truth and the progress of virtue impart.

Antisthenes, at the time he first met Socrates,

---

[5] Original footnote: Xenoph., *Symposium,* IV, § 61-64.

was living at Piraeus, and each day, in order to come and listen to him, he traversed the forty stages that separated him from the city. An irresistible seduction attracted him to his master. "I esteem," he said, "more than any other good, that freedom and leisure that allow me at any moment to see and to hear what most deserves to be seen and to be heard, and to spend my days, in their entirety, in Socrates' presence. Not having a single obol to my name, and being unable to give to Autolycus enough dirt to rub his body with before a contest, nevertheless I can, thanks to Socrates, boast of my opulence. Without intending to, without ever reckoning with me, he gave me infinite gifts, he gave me those riches of the soul that I now take pleasure in sharing with my friends."

How could Socrates not have been attached to him who sought out his dialogs with such ardor and whose strong affection made him jestingly say that he no longer knew whether the love of his disciple was due to earthly Venus or to that celestial Venus who unites souls and inspires them to friendship and virtue. He moreover noticed in him a great ability to bring together men who could be useful to each other and praised that quality in the *good panderer*, that προαγωγεία. Socrates praised the strength of soul and courage of that νόθος [bastard]; while he lamented seeing vanity appear through the holes in Antisthenes' mantle, he could not fail to recognize in him the rare and great qualities that his example had developed in him. The male resignation, the unshakable firmness, that is what Antisthenes most admired in his master; but, less moderate than him, he let himself be carried away by his zeal and arrived at an arrogant severity.

He had been Socrates' disciple for twenty-four years when he saw the latter accused and condemned. He stayed with his master until the very end and was present at those sublime dialogs which [Plato's] *Phædo* has preserved for us the memory of.

Did he then, like Plato, like the other Socratics, seek refuge with Euclid of Megara? We cannot be sure of it. If we are to believe Diogenes Laërtius, he would have been quite happy to avenge his master, to have Anytus banished, and to have Melitus put to death. We cannot lend credence to that tradition, but it needs to be mentioned here to show how famous Antisthenes' attachment to Socrates was.

We have only a small amount of information on Antisthenes' relationships with other disciples of Socrates. He knew Alcibiades and, fully scornful of his conduct, he had attacked him in his works with an extreme violence.

He appears to have been the friend of that currier in the shop where Socrates was pleased to discourse, of that Simon who, the first, collecting the conversations of their common master, edited and published some of the Socratic dialogs.

Plato and Antisthenes always kept at a distance from each other: the Athenian citizen would have had difficulty forgetting that the privileges and renown of his origin placed him at a distance from a νόθος; and his aristocratic tendencies sufficed to sepa-

rate him forever from the philosophy of the
Cynosarges. Their doctrines indicated a more definitive and even deeper opposition; the one attacked, in
the name of experience, the results of Platonic dialectic and denied the existence of ideas; the other found
fault with Antisthenes' opinion on the impossibility
of contradiction; and he who denied contradictions,
being unable to resign himself to support them, wrote
against Plato in the cynical work entitled *Sathon*, a
work that the ancients censured for its impertinence
and coarseness. From that moment on, adds Diogenes
Laërtius, these two philosophers were enemies. From
then on, one understands that Plato contented himself
in his dialogs with making several rare references to
Antisthenes' doctrine, but never mentioned him except with an extreme severity.

Antisthenes had reached the age of maturity without
ceasing to be a disciple [of Socrates], and one must
associate the foundation of the school of Cynicism
with the first years of the fourth century before Jesus
Christ.

The Athenians had erected three gymnasiums,
at the State's expense, and made them available to
youth: the Academy, the Lyceum, and the Cynosarges. They were vast edifices situated outside the
walls of the city and surrounded by gardens and sacred woods. At first consecrated, as their name indicates, to the exercises that make men vigorous and
prepare valiant defenders of the State, the gymnasiums had soon allowed free access to masters who cultivated and enriched their intelligence. The more

progress that the arts and sciences made in Athens, the more instruction that was given in the gymnasiums, and they were witnesses to the noblest efforts and sublimest conquests of the human mind in philosophy. It is there that, far from the tumult of the city, in the shade of the gardens or the porticos, Plato, Antisthenes, and, later, Aristotle conversed with their friends and disciples; a number of youth, pressing around them, thus went from exercises that fortified and embellished their body to studies that limbered up their mind and purified their soul.

But we must distance ourselves now from the Academy and the Lyceum, from those famous and venerated places, and, choosing a more modest task, we will penetrate the Cynosarges to cozy up with Antisthenes.

The Cynosarges was situated on a hill, outside the city, near the road that led to Marathon; its name comes from κυνός ἀργού, white dog; it is reported how a certain Diomus was making a sacrifice to Hercules when a white dog rushed forward, seized the thighs of the victim, and escaped capture by those who were pursuing it. Filled with fear, Diomus consults the oracle who orders him to erect a temple to Hercules, on the very site where the dog had laid its victim down.

The existence of the temple of Cynosarges is attested to by the best authorities; seen there are, in addition, altars to Alcmene, the mother of Hercules; to Hebe, that daughter of Jupiter who later became Hercules' companion; to Iolas, Hercules' nephew who had participated in some of his labors.

The *νόθοι* had sought an asylum in those places consecrated to the son of Jupiter and Alcmene, to a *νόθος* God himself. They got together at the Cynosarges in a gymnasium specially reserved for them; they had their particular cult and their altars; finally, it is there where the tribunal presided who was charged with managing all the affairs that concerned them.

That gymnasium was the only one that had welcomed Antisthenes as a young man, and, when he later wanted to open a school, it was the only one that allowed him to practice and teach. Not long before, under the archontate of Euclid (403, 402 BC), the laws against the *νόθοι,* after having fallen into desuetude in the latter days of Pericles, having been forgotten during the Peloponnesian War, had been reprised in all their rigor; it was once again declared that the child of a foreign mother was nothing but an illegitimate child, and that the *νόθοι* were excluded from religious ceremonies and had no share in the private right of Athenians.

Antisthenes went on, then, to found his school far from the *ἐλεύθεροι*, far from the *ἰθαγενεῖς,* amidst the despised class of men to which he belonged and under the protection of Hercules. That school was called the *Cynosarges school*, or, in other words, the *school of the white dog*, and not long afterwards, the *Cynic school*, or the *school of the dogs*. The name of that gymnasium where Antisthenes taught served to designate his doctrine itself, and it earned him the name of *Απλοκύων*, or *veritable dog*.

Subsequently, Diogenes and his successors

made it a point of honor to be called dogs, *οἱ κύνες*, and justified that name by their brutal and mordant franchise, by their life conformant with nature, by their shamelessness finally. Later, people forgot that the Cynic school was born in the Cynosarges and they willingly supposed that it owed its name to the moral character of its representatives.

When the new Cynics had arrived at those absurdities of behavior that made their school so sadly infamous, they were seen to renounce Antisthenes in some fashion.[6] They attributed the invention of the Cynic life either to Hercules, the God of strength and hard labors, or to Diogenes, that "Socrates gone mad."

But while it is curious to accept the tradition that separates Antisthenes from the other Cynics, and which elevates him above them and associates him with Socrates, one must, however, with ancient au-

---

[6]Original footnote: Diogenes boasted about modeling his life on that of Hercules (Laërt., VI, 71); he imitates the animals as well. – Crates says he is a citizen of Diogenes (ib., 93). – The Sophists who wrote letters under the names of these two philosophers did not neglect a rather characteristic trait: "It is not at all Antisthenes who first gave me these teachings," said the Pseudo-Diogenes (ep. 5, P. 240, Boiss.); "I attribute them to the gods, to the heroes, and to those poets who have guided Greece toward wisdom, Homer, and the tragedians." The Pseudo-Crates says that Diogenes achieved and accomplished what Antisthenes had only begun (ep. 6, p. 91, Commel.); that the Cynic philosophy did not exist before Diogenes, that Diogenes is its founder (ep. 2, p. 17; ep. 5, p. 21, 22, Boiss.). – Œnomaus maintains that the Cynic philosophy is not from Antisthenes, nor from Diogenes... and he adds that the most remarkable representatives of that school thought that Hercules, to whom we owe so much gratitude, had also given the example of the Cynic lifestyle. Julian, Orat. VI, p. 187.

thors, acknowledge him as the veritable founder of the Cynic school. His doctrine, vaster and more scientific in fact than that of his successors, encompassed all the ideas that they exposed and later developed; if they had the merit of presenting, under a surprising and new form, some of his opinions, if on certain topics they gave more precision and force to his thought, they too often made the mistake of exaggerating him, and they went to excesses that Antisthenes would have reproached them for.

If we come to consider his life, he stands out by his calm resignation, his firmness, and his self-severity; one no longer knows whether he was born poor or whether he had voluntarily chosen poverty, the better to practice virtue; whether his birth had reduced him to the Cynosarges or whether he came on his own accord to seek out great examples and to bring consolation to those who were suffering; he finds pleasure celebrating the advantages of poverty and an obscure condition. It is because of them that he learned to detach himself from all those possessions that men's vanity and folly strive to acquire, that he lived free and independent, and that he knew the price of virtue and had tasted all the pleasures of it. Thus, what seems to others hard necessity, against which their entire soul revolts, he turned into a merit and a glory by supporting it; what appears to them as a bad thing, his noble pride accepts as a good.

But it is not enough for him to be poor; he wants to appear so. For a long time before [his time], the *tribonium*, that coat made of coarse fabric and dark color, had been abandoned for finer fabric and more sumptuous clothing whose fashion foreigners had brought with them to Athens. Some old men had vainly tried to resist the general enthusiasm; the poor alone had held on to that ancient and simple dress. Antisthenes wore a previously-worn *tribonium*, through the holes of which his vanity showed; he renounced even the usage of the tunic, and he was the first to throw over his left shoulder an extent of that mantle which, thus folded over and falling behind, was supposed to wrap him completely and keep him from the cold. He seeks to attract glances, to surprise by his appearance and his behavior, and in his very simplicity his pride shines out. Thus was the obligatory costume prepared, the strange accoutrement of the Cynics.[7]

By his doctrine and by the example of his life, he is, then, the true leader of the Cynic school; an attentive study of his philosophy and his behavior provides the secret behind all the great ideas and noble actions that the history of his school presents, and when we see it veer from the truth and exceed all measure, we can see therein the excesses and aberrations of his successors.

Does it not seem as though his disciples ought to have pressed up around that man who had lived for so many years in Socrates' company and who had so

---

[7]Original footnote: Diocles. (ap. Laërt., VI, 13), Apuleus (*Apolog.*, p. 58, Panck.), Lucian (*Dial.* XI) says that Antisthenes carried the stick and satchel. All this part of tradition is very confused, and one has too often ascribed to Antisthenes the ideas and usages of other Cynics. Nothing proves that he ever begged.

profoundly penetrated his doctrine and spoke of virtue and the true good with so much force and originality? Did he not also make himself known by a rare facility to dispose the minds of those who were listening to him to his will, to lead them by conversations full of charm to the end that he proposed for them? Thus, to the interest of his doctrine was joined the resources of his mind and a talent for speaking.

But to whom did he address himself? To the νόθοι who were hardly interested in philosophy, hardly motivated to resign themselves and seek a consolation in haughty disdain for the goods and pleasures that their birth had refused to them. The Athenians did not frequent the Cynosarges at all, and if they sometimes came to hear Antisthenes, that virtue that he taught and practiced was nothing to them but the arrogance of a poor man and a νόθος; those proud maxims that emanated from the Cynosarges could arouse their curiosity, but not trouble them in the middle of their voluptuous life, in the sweet possession of their wealth and privileges.

Antisthenes attempts a great moral reform: he wants to lead man to virtue by privations and hard work, by detaching him from all possessions and pleasures. He does not compare himself to a physician who, by his able care, maintains health, but to someone who proposes violent remedies for serious maladies; he employs fire and iron. The more softness and laxity he sees around him, the more he insists on energy, effort, and struggle against oneself.

Finally, the severity of his character corresponds with the rigid principles of his ethics: he roughly treats those who pretend to attach themselves to him; and when he is asked why he has so few disciples, "it is because," he says, "I chase them away with the whip of Corcyra."

Of Antisthenes' disciples, Diogenes is the only one whom history mentions. He is a man with a not terribly cultivated intelligence, but of a mind replete with finesse and vivacity, whom an extreme energy distinguishes; he is also surprising by his sharp revilement, his violent attacks against all defects of character and vices, and by his austerity, the rigor of his conduct.

Diogenes natural qualities were developed under powerful influences. Chased out of Sinope, his birth city, for having counterfeited money with his father, he came to find refuge in Greece and lived in extreme destitution in the midst of opulent Athens. Taken by pirates, he was subsequently sold by them and ended up in slavery. As he tells it, all the imprecations of the tragedians fell on him: the more rudely fate struck him, the more he retreats into himself, closes himself off in proud contempt for what he no longer possesses and the independent possession of real goods.

Antisthenes was a *νόθος*; Diogenes was an exile, a mendicant, a slave; Antisthenes exaggerated Socrates' doctrines; Diogenes will exaggerate those of Antisthenes even more. He finds his master too weak, too indulgent for his taste and accuses him of lacking, in his conduct, any semblance of the loftiness of his principles. "You are like," he told him, "the trumpet that makes beautiful sounds but does not hear them itself."

Antisthenes, taken aback by so complete a candor and so ample an ardor, responds simply by saying to him: "And you, how are you not like the wasps whose wings make so little noise and whose stinger is so piercing?" He could not help admiring Diogenes' rigid character and male virtue; but that zeal that he himself had excited [in him], he sought vainly to temper it and regretted being unable to moderate its excesses. A new age was beginning for Cynic philosophy, and Antisthenes, before passing away, witnessed that transformation of the school that he had founded. He left no disciple who was truly faithful to his doctrine, and Diogenes was the leader of a renewed and degenerate Cynicism.

Antisthenes died in Athens, following a long illness, around the year 365 BC.

Needless to say, this is not the moment for us to judge that philosopher, but from the facts that we have exposed, several reflections stand out that are important to gather.

Over the course of a long life, Antisthenes saw Athens during several very different epochs, the most curious and perhaps the most instructive ones in its history.

He saw his country during the most beautiful days of its glory, and he had witnessed all the vicissitudes of the Peloponnesian War. After having fought so many glorious battles, Athens fell into the hands of the Spartans. The Thirty Tyrants made fifteen hundred citizens perish; they struck Theramenes himself, too just and too moderate a man to be associated with their violences.

To the government of Pericles succeeded the misfortunes of a turbulent democracy: the rich were pursued, the best citizens were proscribed, and accusations of impiety unjustly multiplied; Anaxagoras who was the first to have spoken about God and Providence was obliged to flee Athens; Socrates, the wisest of men, died for the holiest of causes, bequeathing to his disciples the tradition of his admirable doctrine.

When the most flourishing of States thus succumbs, and when, for particular individuals, wealth, credit, and virtue are reasons for exile and even death, is not the wisest person someone who, taking stock of himself, scorns all external goods and lifts himself above the blows of fortune through indifference and insensibility?

During Antisthenes' life, literature and the arts shined with the most brilliant splendor; but also ambition, love of wealth, a taste for luxury and softness, a thirst for pleasure, the depravation of morals, all made rapid progress. Was there not also a lesson there for the wise man, and would it not have led him to scorn what others sought with such ardor, to be content with what is necessary, and to love privations even?

Such is the violent reaction that tempted the Cynic school and continued in the Stoic school. The closer ancient civilization and ancient society approaches their dissolution and ruin, the more arrogant the maxims of those philosophers who seek to rehabilitate hard work and toil, proscribing all pleasures and all possessions, and wanting virtue alone to be the goal of our actions; exaggerated doctrine, impotent effort of several strongly-tempered souls, inaccessible consolation for the rest of us mortals!

Chapter 2: Antisthenes' Works

Antisthenes' works were remarkable both for the interest and importance of the doctrines they contained and the charm of their style. They acquainted the philosophers of Greece and Rome, and later the Fathers of the Church, with one of the most illustrious disciples of Socrates, the founder of the Cynic school, the precursor of Stoicism; writers admired them, rhetors and grammarians studied them as one of the most perfect models of Attic language.

Let us not forget that, before having grown attached to Socrates, Antisthenes had been a disciple of the Sophists. Whereas Gorgias was applauded for a studied eloquence, and a figurative and pretentious style, Prodicus had provided to the language, to philosophy even I might say, real services, by applying himself to determining the precise meaning of words.

Their lessons and examples were not at all lost on Antisthenes; in his choice of expressions he was guided not only by natural taste, but also by a thoughtful familiarity with the resources of the language. Habituated to declamations and oratorical exercises, he loved their rich style and sustained eloquence; his dialogs recall the manner of his first masters, but one recognized that same manner principally in his work *On Virtue* and in the *Exhortations*.

If he had preserved their qualities, it is to be believed that he modified their style and tempered their defects. The importance and elevation of ideas that are familiar to us, do they not decide our style? How could the admirer and disciple of Socrates, the founder of one of the great moral schools of antiquity, not have developed his own way of thinking and writing? The art of the Sophists did not appear in him except with a wisdom and a measure unknown to them; a happy accord, a perfect harmony of brilliant and solid qualities, assured for his writings a distinguished rank among the literary and philosophical works of Greece.

Writers, rhetors, grammarians, lexicographers, all attentively noted the expressions employed by Antisthenes; one can cite Athenaeus, Erotianus, Pollux, Photius and the Scholiasts. Aristotle borrows an example of comparison from Antisthenes works; and Demetrius of Phalerum, in order to establish the rules of construction, gives a passage by Antisthenes as his model.

Dionysius of Halicarnassus, while listing the great writers who lived at the time of Thucydides, and who, as witnesses like him of the Peloponnesian War, could write about its history, gives the names of the orators Andocide, Antiphon, and Lysias; and cites, among the Socratic philosophers, Antisthenes together with Critias and Xenophon.

Epictetus and Fronton compare Antisthenes' style to that of Plato and Xenophon, Longinus likens him to Plato, Xenophon, and Aeschines; among the works that he proposes as rules, types, and models of true Attic style, Phrynichus mentions the writings of Antisthenes and particularly, for their perfect correctness and purity of expression, his *Cyrus* and his work on *Odysseus*; he puts Antisthenes on the same level as Plato, Demosthenes, Thucydides, Xenophon, Aeschines the Socratic, Critias, Aristophanes, Aeschylus, Sophocles, and Euripides.

If we consider, on the other hand, the philosophical merit of Antisthenes' work, they are, in the eyes of one of the most authentic among the ancients, one of the most precious monuments of Socrates' teachings; and from that point of view, Panetius could compare them only to the works of Plato, Xenophon, and Aeschines.

But to speak only of the things that are his own, one recognizes in his work that quality of the *good panderer* which Socrates attributes to him in Xenophon's *Symposium;* Xenophon himself says that Antisthenes was extremely agreeable in his conversations; the historian Theopompus also praises in him that fine and penetrating mind which, by the hability and charm of his discourse, knows how to lead others to the goal that he proposes; and to confirm the authority of Xenophon and Theopompus, Diogenes Laërtius invoked a more direct and more convincing testimony, – that of Antisthenes' works themselves.

Cicero, all the while recognizing in these works more intelligence than instruction, enjoyed reading them; Aulus-Gellius placed Antisthenes alongside Socrates and Plato; Lucian estimated his writings to be on the same level as those of the leader of the Academy; Diogenes Laërtius pointed out the similarity that existed among all these minds: "Among all the philosophers who go by the name of

Socratic, there are three, he said, who hold the first
rank: Plato, Xenophon, Antisthenes."

The celebrated historian from Chios, Theopompus, whom we have already cited, went further:
he put Antisthenes above all the other Socratics and
accused Plato of having stolen many of his dialogs;
Pasiphon of Eretria, on the other hand, took Antisthenes for a model and classified his own productions
among those of the master whom he believed he had
imitated. He had introduced forgeries among the
works of Aeschines and many other authors: he published the *Little Cyrus*, the *Little Hercules*, and the
Alcibiades under Antisthenes' name.

The great number of testimonies, which we
have just now presented, and the merit of some of
them, leave no doubt as to the high esteem in which
the ancients held Antisthenes' work; they admired
them equally from a literary point of view as from a
philosophical point of view, and if time had not destroyed them, if they should ever see the light of day
again, we shall have perhaps several more master-
pieces among the writings of the Attics and certainly
a precious philosophical collection to join to those of
Plato and Xenophon.

Ethics and politics, logic and rhetoric, physics
and religious exegesis, commentaries on the poets,
Antisthenes had written on the widest variety of subjects. His works were very numerous; they were dis-
tributed in ten tomes, and Diogenes Laërtius left us a
long catalog of them. But he had doubtless reproduced, without verifying, the list that he found in
some treatise on the Socratics, and he did not even

make an effort to remove the works that, in his own view, passed for apocryphal. Fortunately, his testimony is often confirmed by that of other authors, and therefore we can arrive at certain facts about many writings of Cynic philosophy.

Antisthenes had written, on moral questions, a rather large number of works inspired by the teaching of Socrates and whose subjects, often even whose titles, recalled the dialogs of other Socratics.

In the first rank must be placed that which was entitled *Hercules*; for no other work of his had more importance or fame. But a difficulty presents itself now: Diogenes Laërtius, in his catalog, indicates three works bearing the name of *Hercules*, in tome IV: *Ἡρακλῆς ὁ μείζων ἢ περὶ ἰσχύος*; in tome X: *Ἡρακλῆς ἢ Μίδας* and *Ἡρακλῆς ἢ περὶ φρονήσεως ἢ ἰσχύος*.

If three dialogs by Antisthenes, or only two even, bore the name of *Hercules* in their title, how could it be that Eratosthenes, Plutarch, Proclus and Diogenes Laërtius himself, cited simply *Hercules*? Would they not have taken care to distinguish between these different works and designated precisely which one of them they quoted from?

Diogenes Laërtius himself informs us that Pasiphon of Eretria had supposed, and introduced, among the works of Antisthenes one *Ἡρακλῆς ἐλάσσων*. That supposed dialog was doubtless *Ἡρακλῆς ἢ Μίδας*.

But the two other titles, do they not have a striking resemblance to each other? Are they really two distinct subjects? Prudence and the strength of soul, such as Antisthenes understands them, do they not go hand in hand, and could he, in the first work, treat of *ἰσχύς* [strength] without speaking about *φρόνησις* [prudence], which is the indispensable condition of it? It is probable that the same writing by Antisthenes figures twice in the catalog, which Pasiphon of Eretria had altered the title of in tome IV, substituting *ὁ μείζων* for the words *ἢ περὶ φρονήσεως,* and which, later, those who had the treatise in hand clumsily reintroduced into tome X the exact and complete title of, which they no longer found in tome IV.

If we consider the fragments that have come down to us, it seems to me that their similarities, the facility by which they come together on their own, testify to the unity of the work that our thought can reconstitute.

The title reveals to us the subject of the work.

Antisthenes discusses therein the strength of the soul, *ἰσχύς,* the supreme virtue that Hercules was the model and practically the personification of.

The strength of the soul has its source in reflection, in the wise man's thought, in the spirit of prudence, *φρόνησις.*

It maintains itself and grows by experience and struggle, and by hard work and toil, which are from then on a good.

To develop in ourselves that mind of prudence, to seek out struggle and toil, means to develop ourselves in virtue, in the strength of the soul, through all our thoughts and all our actions; it is in this way that virtue is learnt.

Little do other goods matter, exterior goods, and, for example, the praises that are made to us.

The supreme good, the goal of humanity, is to live in conformance with virtue.

Such were, in themselves, and in their strict liaison, the principle doctrines put forward by Antisthenes in his *Hercules*.

Thus, to honor the God of the Cynosarges, the God of *νόθοι,* the God of toil and hard work, Antisthenes presented him as a model in the work wherein he exposed the most essential principles of his moral doctrine. Desirous perhaps to surpass Prodicus and to make the famous declamation of the Sophist be forgotten, he made Hercules himself speak, and, as if the hero had been inspired in advance of that lofty philosophy that had descended for the first time on earth, he lent him the wisdom and genius of Socrates.

Antisthenes made use of a tradition that made Hercules a disciple of Chiron and the centaur a habile sage to instruct and form others. Hercules, having arrived in Chiron's cave, had respected his life; full of admiration for him, full of love for his wisdom, he had collected his teachings and did not leave Pelion until after having witnessed the death of his master. Later he transmitted to his children the useful lessons and wise counsels that he had faithfully guarded the memory of.

Hercules was not the only work in which Antisthenes had developed this thesis that summarizes

his ethic: "hard work, toil is a good." The teachings
that his life had furnished him, the life of a Greek
hero, he sought them also among the barbarians and,
like Xenophon, he proposed Cyrus as a model.

Diogenes Laërtius in tome IV of his catalog
cites: Κῦρος, and in the 5th: Κῦρος ἢ περὶ βασιλείας;
an indication confirmed by Atheneus who distinguishes two *Cyrus,* and by the most formal testimony
of Cicero who designates the very volume in which
they were found. Let us remark however that Cicero
does not seem to consider the two *Cyrus* as two different works, but like two books of the same work,
and that Phrynichus says simply *The Cyrus,* without
distinguishing the two conversations that form, in his
view, a complete whole.

When Diogenes Laërtius reports that Pasiphon
of Eretria considers the *Little Cyrus* to be Antisthenes', he does not talk about one of the two dialogs
inscribed in tomes IV and V; but, rather, about Κῦρος
ἢ ἐρώμενος or Κῦρος ἢ κατάσκοποι contained in the
Xth [tome] together with other apocryphal writings.

Cicero and Phrynichus do not leave us any
doubt about the literary merit of the two dialogs
which had *Cyrus* for a title. Unfortunately, there is no
fragment of any importance that remains, no evidence
that permits us to reconstitute its doctrine and appreciate its worth. All that we have is this beautiful
phrase: "O Cyrus, it is the right of kings to be accused
for the good that they have done"; and we know, on
the other hand, that one of those dialogs contained violent accusations, bitter invectives, directed at Alcibiades.

Let us cite, in the third place, the three books of *Exhortations* (t. II), which had justice and strength of soul for their object: περὶ δικαιοσύνης καὶ ἀνδρείας προτρεπτικὸς πρῶτος, δεύτερος, τρίτος. The merits of its style, the charms of its composition make it one of the most remarkable writings by Antisthenes, one of those that recalled the manner of his first teachers; a large number of ancient authors have also mentioned its elegant and refined expressions; unfortunately, the fragments that have come down to us hold no interest for philosophy.

Beyond these writings, for which the testimony by Diogenes Laërtius is confirmed by other authorities, his catalog signals still more works relative to ethics, and here are their titles:

On the Strength of the Soul, περὶ ἀνδρείας (t. III).

On the Good, περὶ ἀγαθόῦ (t. III).

On Law or On the Beautiful and the Just, περὶ νόμου ἢ περὶ καλοῦ καὶ δικαίου (t. III). One has to think that, in it, Antisthenes established, according to Socrates' example, the identity of the beautiful and the good, and the dependence of the written law on eternal and immutable justice.

On Injustice and Impiety, περὶ ἀδικίας καὶ ἀσεβείας (t. VIII); perhaps he identified them as well and showed that to act in conformity with virtue is to obey God's commands and honor him thereby.

One could include in this same class the treatise *On Pleasure*, περὶ ἡδονῆς (t. VIII) and the περὶ παιδοποίας ἢ περὶ γάμου ἐρωτικός (t. II).

Such were the writings by Antisthenes that
dealt directly with ethics. Political science, immediate
application of the first, and to which Plato,
Xenophon, and other Socratic philosophers consecrated so many and such brilliant works, had not at all
been neglected by Antisthenes, and the catalog by
Diogenes Laërtius presents the following titles:

On Law and On the State, περὶ νόμου ἢ περὶ
πολιτείας (t. III). It is probably the πολιτικὸς διάλογος
which contains, according to Athenaeus, a violent cri-
tique of all the Athenian demagogues.

περὶ νόμου ἢ περὶ καλοῦ καὶ δικαίου, and
Κῦρος ἢ περὶ βασιλείας, – dialogs mentioned earlier.

Menexenus or On Leadership, Μενέξενος ἢ
περὶ τοῦ ἄρχειν (t. X).

On Victory, περί νίκης, οἰκονομικός [sic] (t.
III).

On Freedom and Slavery, περὶ ἐλευθερίας καὶ
δουλείας (t . III).

Several works by Antisthenes belonged to that part of
philosophy that the Greeks called physics.

On going through Diogenes Laërtius' list, at
first we notice the general treatises on the nature of
beings: περὶ φύσεως α' β' (t. VII) followed by
ερώτημα περὶ φύσεως.

The περὶ φύσεως is certainly the same work as

Physicus [On Physics] cited by Cicero and by Lactantius, wherein Antisthenes put the Socratic principle of divine unity in opposition to the plurality of gods, to the variety of religions and superstitions of the people. One has the right to suppose, by analogy, that Clement of Alexandria and Theodoret drew from it the texts wherein Antisthenes formally affirms the spirituality of divine nature and the impossibility of knowing and representing it through material images.

Moreover, we note these special works:

On the Nature of Animals, περὶ ζώων φύσως (t. II).

On Physiognomy, περὶ τῶν σοφιστῶν φυσιο-γνωμονικός (t. II). Athenaeus cites: Antisthenes, ἐν τῷ φυσιογνωμονικῷ, but the passage that he brings our attention to is insignificant and does not help in understanding how a treatise on physiognomy is related to the Sophists.

Finally, the writings *On Life, Death, and the Hells*, περὶ ζωῆς καὶ θανάτου , περὶ τοῦ ἀποθανεῖν, περὶ τῶν ἐν Ἀδου (t. VII).

Almost all the treatises in tomes VI and VII, and many others even, had to do with logic, rhetoric, and grammar.

The works on logic were, according to Diogenes Laërtius, as follows:

A dialog *On Truth*, Ἀλήθεια (t. VII), one of those which, according to the testimony of the same author, by its investigation and the elegance of its style, reminds one of the manner of rhetors and even that of Gorgias.

Four books *On Opinion and Science*, περὶ δόξης καὶ ἐπιστήμης α' β' γ' δ' (t. VII), wherein he opposes absolute certainty and immutable science to ever-changing opinions, undoubtedly in alignment with Socrates, and which he had spoken about in the preceding dialog.

The treatise *On Opinions or the Disputer*, δόξαι ἢ ἐριστικός (t. VII).

Three dialogs entitled *Sathon or On Contradiction*, Σάθων ἢ περὶ τοῦ ἀντιλέγειν α' β' γ' (t. VI). Athenaeus, who refers to this work by the name of *Sathon*, says that it was directed against Plato, and reproaches Antisthenes for the invectives and coarseness that he found in it. One may ascribe to this dialog several fragments by Antisthenes relative to Plato's opinions. Diogenes Laërtius informs us that it was written following a discussion in which the latter had argued with Antisthenes over the possibility of contradiction. Later on, I will show the meaning of and importance for Antisthenes of this doctrine on the impossibility of contradictions.

Two dialogs on dialectic procedures in which he probably revealed the Socratic method of discussion and investigation, περὶ τοῦ διαλέγεθαι ἀντιλογικός and περὶ διαλέκτου (t. VI). Comparable to it is the περὶ ἐρωτήσεως καὶ ἀποκρίσεως (t. VII); finally, περὶ τοῦ μανθάνειν προβλήματα (t. VII).

Two treatises on persuasion were related to

rhetoric: περὶ τοῦ ἐπιτρόπου ἢ περὶ τοῦ πείθεσθαι, περὶ πίστεως (t. III).

Grammar had, in Antisthenes' eyes, a huge importance; for him, "the determination of the meaning of words was the very principle of all instruction"; that is probably the opinion that he expressed in the five books *On Instruction or Categories, περὶ παιδείας ἢ περὶ ὀνομάτων, α' β' γ' δ' ε'* (t. VII) and in an analogous treatise, *On the Use of Categories or the Disputer, περὶ ὀνομάτων χρήσεως ἢ ἐριστικός* (ib.); let us categorize them in the same series as περὶ λέξεως ἢ περὶ χαρακτήρων (t. I).[8]

Such were the philosophical works of Antisthenes: in their entirety, they addressed, as one can see, all the great questions that human thought might pose; they simultaneously embraced all objects of knowledge, God, nature, and man; and if ethics was the most important, in his eyes, of all the bodies of knowledge, he did not try to shut himself up in it and to despise other parts of philosophy and science.

The catalog given by Diogenes Laërtius presents the titles of a large number of works related to Homer; thus, Antisthenes is often cited by the Scholiasts; and Dio Chrysostom included him among the poet's interpreters.

He often spoke about the folly of men who be-

---

[8]Original footnote: Socrates and his disciples did not neglect grammatical investigations; it is what the dialogs περὶ γραμμάτων by Crito and Simmias (Laërt., II, 121, 124) and the περὶ ἐπῶν by Simmias (ib., 124) prove.

lieve they know and understand all that they have confided to their memory or to their tablets; and, in Xenophon's *Symposium*, when Nikeratos boasts about having learnt by heart all the lines of Homer, he enjoys confounding him by mockery: "The rhapsodists," he said to him, "are they not the most inept of men? They go reciting the *Iliad* and the *Odyssey*, but are, as Socrates remarks, incapable of explaining its meaning." Thus condemning that sterile admiration for Homer's poetry, Antisthenes attempted to interpret them from both the religious and the moral points of view.

They were the vastest collection of mythological traditions; and their religious character had for a long time made them sacred in the eyes of the Greeks. But the age that had inspired them were gone; reason had taken the place of imagination, science that of poetry; myths had been succeeded by philosophy which, seeking to account for all things, had interpreted the myths themselves, and destroyed national religion while pretending to explain it.

Later we will see, when we treat of Antisthenes' physics, that, like Xenophon and Anaxagoras, he openly discussed popular beliefs and religious institutions. Not only is his revilement against priests and the mysteries cited: Clement of Alexandria, the rhetor [Aelius] Aristides, and the Scholiasts borrowed from his works on Homer and have preserved for us some rather curious examples of his philosophical exegesis.

In one of his principle dialogs, in order to give more interest and credit to his ideas on the nature of the good, he associated them with traditions related to Hercules, and to the centaur Chiron. Julian[9] informs us that he loved to present the myths in that way, in support of his doctrine, and that his works were worthy of serving as models to those who, in the exposition of his moral philosophy, want to make use of fictions and allegories.

These procedures of discussion and interpretation were familiar [to readers] in his works on Homer; and thus, at the same time that he openly expressed his opinion on the origin and value of religious traditions, he exposed his philosophic ideas in a new and attractive manner.

On the other hand, Socrates' pupil, the philosopher who sought everywhere for truths useful to man, could study the depiction of characters and passions in the Homeric poems and gather teachings and maxims from them.

Many passages preserved by the Scholiasts give evidence that Antisthenes also had taken up this point of view. He showed, for example, that the epithet πολύτροπος can designate a quality or a defect, the reflective and resourceful mind of a wise man whom no difficulty surprises, whom no event catches off guard, but also, among evil people, that mind of ruse and duplicity which is the opposite of the wisdom of Nestor, the openness of Agamemnon, the loyalty of Achilles. When Calypso, in order to retain Ulysses, promises him immortality, Antisthenes remarks how many deceitful hopes and false promises

---

[9]Julian: potentially Julian the Apostate (AD 331-363), also known as Julian the Philosopher.

love gives rise to.

Thus, in these writings by Antisthenes one recognized the work of a philosopher; he considered Homer a sage who at one moment expresses his true thoughts while at another, conforming to popular beliefs, cloaks it under veils and in allegory; and he showed that truth and opinion had alternately inspired him. Nothing then is more different than the commentaries composed by grammarians and rhetors. Antisthenes, moreover, was not constrained to follow the poet in order to explain each of his thoughts successively; he also had not expounded in a complete treatise a system of discussion and exegesis; he had merely chosen several interesting points, presented some interpretative essays, some philosophical studies on Homer.

Consequently, one cannot be surprised by the large number of works on Homer included in Diogenes Laërtius' catalog; they occupy a part of the tomes I and VIII, and the entirety of the IXth under the following titles:

περὶ Ὁμήρου [On Homer] (t. VIII); it is perhaps the treatise wherein, as Dio Chrysostom describes it, he showed that the poetry often expressed virtue, but often also showed conformance to vulgar opinions.

περὶ Ὀδυσσείας [On Odysseus] (t. IX).

Ὀδυσσεὺς ἢ περὶ Ὀδυσσέως [Odysseus or On Odysseus] (t. I): perhaps it is necessary to add to this work the long scholia on the character of Ulysses, on the subject of the word πολύτροπος [versatile].

Κύκλωψ ἢ περὶ Ὀδυσσέως [Cyclops or On Odysseus] (t. IX). The Scholiast appears to have had that work at hand.

περὶ οἴνου χρήσεως ἢ περὶ μέθης ἢ περὶ τοῦ Κύκλωπος [On Wine, or Drunkenness, or On the Cyclops] (ib.), work cited by the rhetor [Aelius] Aristides.

περὶ Κίρκης [On Circe] (ib.).

περὶ τῆς ῥάβδου [On Circe's Wand] (ib.); on Circe's enchanted wand.

περὶ Ὀδυσσέως καὶ Πηνελόπης [On Odysseus and Penelope] (ib.).

περὶ τοῦ κυνός (ib.); on the dog Argus who alone recognized his master.

περὶ Ἑλένης καὶ Πηνελόπης [On Helen and Penelope] (ib.).

Ἀθηνᾶ ἢ περὶ Τηλεμάχου [Athena or On Telemachus] (ib.); doubtless the Scholiast had borrowed from this work the passage wherein Antisthenes attributes to Minerva something like the personification of wisdom.

περὶ Πρωτέως [On Proteus] (ib.).

περὶ Ἀμφιαράου [On Amphiaraus] (ib.).

περὶ Κάλχαντος [On Calchas] (t. VIII).

Αἴας ἢ Αἴαντος λόγος [Ajax or About Ajax] (t. I).

Ὀρέστου ἀπολογία ἢ περὶ τῶν δικογράφων

[Orestes' Apologia or On Legal Documents...] (t. I).

The critics believe that we must group the other works of tome VIII into this same category: περὶ ἀδικίας καὶ ἀσεβείας [On Injustice and Impiety], περὶ κατασκόπου [On Espionage], περὶ ἡδονῆς [On Hedonism], finally the general treatise περὶ ἐξηγητῶν [On Scholiasts or Interpreters] (t. VIII), wherein he doubtless criticized vulgar commentaries.

The topics of these writings are almost all taken from the *Odyssey*, that is, the poem in which Homer had depicted, not so much the life of battle camps anymore, but human life with all its vicissitudes and all its battles.

Clearly Diogenes Laërtius' catalog is not absolutely trustworthy: questionable works may have been included in it, and among numerous variants two titles could have easily been combined to make one, or vice versa a complex title could have been admitted as several different works.

But the evidence by Dio, the περὶ οἴνου χρήσεως [On the Use of Wine] cited by Aristides, and passages by the Scholiasts, all give reason to believe that the treatises by Antisthenes were numerous and contained isolated discussions on different points of the Homeric poems.

They are all lost. Actually, two declamations have been preserved for us under Antisthenes' name: the discourse of Ajax and the discourse of Ulysses, disputing Achille's arms between them.

If they were actually written by him, we must

regret that the most insignificant works of his were the only ones that time had spared. Not one work containing his philosophical thought has been discovered, not one personal opinion, not one interpretation of the Homeric traditions. They are not the essays of a philosopher who seeks the religious and moral meaning of celebrated poems, but the exercises of some rhetor, the μελεταί [exercises] on a given theme.

Diogenes Laërtius said that Antisthenes had written two books on Theognis [of Megara], περὶ Θέογνιδος δ' έ (t. II).

Finally, let us cite also the work περὶ μουσικῆς [On Music] (t. VIII); music and poetry, are they not sisters? And do not rhapsodes sing the *Iliad* and the *Odyssey*? We have, therefore, a certain right to place, together with Diogenes Laërtius, that treatise of Antisthenes' beside his works on Homer.

Such are the four great classes into which Antisthenes' works may be categorized: ethics, physics, logic, – all the fundamental questions of philosophy that are thus found in that vast collection: the interpretation of Homer is, at one and the same time, the application and confirmation of that philosophy.

What is more, Diogenes Laërtius' catalog presents some choice words aimed at Antisthenes' contemporaries.

The work on Aspasia, Ασπασια (t. V), is also cited by Athenaeus, and we know from him that Aspasia, Pericles, and their sons were violently accused by Antisthenes.

We have already seen that the authenticity of *Alcibiades* was contested, and that it was attributed to Pasiphon of Eretria. That work is cited only in the catalog by Diogenes Laërtius (t. X), and the silence of other ancient writers is all the more remarkable given that they often invoke the testimony Antisthenes against Alcibiades. Athenaeus, the only person who designated the work that he drew from, cited one of the two *Cyrus*.

What is certain is that Antisthenes had put to-gether the gravest accusations against Alcibiades in his writings; in them, the Cynic's license was beyond measure; blaming, in energetic terms, Alcibiades' conduct and shameless pleasures, he accused him of having made accomplices of his dissolutions and de-baucheries the very people whom nature made it a law for him to respect. Nonetheless, that hatred of his for Alcibiades, that indignation that spared neither him nor his family, doubtless had its explanation and its blameless origins in the conscience of Socrates' disciple. Alcibiades had given Athens an example of every imaginable disorder, and he had had the most harmful influence on Greek mores; but his brilliant qualities and often honest actions made his too public immorality almost forgotten; he had astonished by his virtues no less than his vices. In political life, if he had taken the upper hand over the Athenians, it was to their detriment; when exile followed his hopes for conquest and glory, he conspired against the father-land, and then, as if surprised by himself, he sought to deflect the evils that he had brought down on it. Thus, ever ready to interpret every role with equal success, always in opposition to himself, he reunited in the highest degree the qualities of the Sophist. How to recognize in him a disciple and friend of Socrates? Or rather, as the Athenians say, what to think of someone who had made [of him] such an enemy of the state, ethics, and the Gods? More than any other person, Alcibiades contributed to conflating Socrates, in the eyes of the people, with the despised race of the Sophists, and, by accrediting that fatal error, he prepared the condemnation and death of his teacher. Hence that profound hatred of Alcibiades by the Socratics, hatred which the writings of Aeschines no less than those of Antisthenes gave witness to.

This latter had written against Isocrates, apropos of his ἀμάρτυρον, and perhaps also against Lysias. But Diogenes Laërtius is the sole authority here, and his highly altered text leaves doubts about both the title and the number even of the works (t. I).

Finally, Antisthenes had attacked Gorgias in a dialog entitled Ἀρχέλαος [Archelaus] (t. X), dialog in which he appears to have entrusted to the famous disciple of Anaxagoras the task of combatting the Sophists who had vilified and prostituted wisdom and knowledge.

Such were the works of Antisthenes: after having classified them in this way, it will not be without interest to investigate under what influences they were composed and how they reflect the development of his mind.

Gorgias and the other Sophists inspired in him a taste for the rich and harmonious style that always

distinguished his writings. Although he knew how to
resist the influence of those who taught him how to
maintain opposing arguments with equal success, although he later argued against them, no one can deny
that some of his works recall their teachings and,
above all, the grammatical investigations of Prodicus;
such as περὶ λέξεως ἢ περὶ χαρακτήρων [On Words or
On Characters], περὶ τοῦ διαλέγεσθαι [On Dialog],
περὶ διαλέκτου [On Dialect], περὶ παιδείας ἢ
ὀνομάτων [On Education or Names], περὶ ὀνομάτων
χρήσεως [On the Use of Names]. Perhaps he owed to
them his appreciation for Homer and learned to understand and admire him together with those who
were often inspired[, as he was,] in the reading of his
poems.

Archelaus is the work of the disillusioned disciple, of Antisthenes having become a student of
Socrates, and it is undoubtedly necessary to compare
it to περὶ τῶν σοφιστῶν φυσιογνωμονικός [On the
Physiognomy of the Sophists] and his works on the
impossibility of contradictions.

With Socrates, Antisthenes learned how to
temper his investigation of style and trained himself
in simplicity and moderation, which his previous
teachers were unable to instruct him in. He sought to
imitate in his writings the format of those able conversations by which Socrates confidently led souls to
the goal that he had marked out in advance. We can
affirm that the Exhortations, Politics, Cyrus, Truth,
Sathon were dialogs; Diogenes Laërtius and Panetius
seem even to designate all the works by Antisthenes
as dialogs. On perusing the list of his writings on

ethics, was no one was struck by the traces that Socrates' lessons had left? What topics were treated that Antisthenes hadn't heard his master discuss many times? I need but a single proof: they are the numerous, permanent similarities among the titles of those works and the subjects treated by the other Socratics. The effort that I have taken to indicate in my notes the dialogs of Simon, of Simmias, of Phaedo, of Crito, of Aeschines have exempted me from having to insist on that point.

In his just recognition and admiration for the person to whom he owed the riches of his soul, Antisthenes was pleased to give to Socrates a place in his works and to entrust to him the principle role in his dialogs; he proposed him as a model, he vaunted his counsels, he celebrated his virtues and, above all, that strength of soul that would suffice for us to be happy if we possessed it in the same degree as he did. He recalled also the courage that Socrates had shown in his battles and the rights that he had acquired through valor. When Athenaeus seeks to prove that Socrates never carried any weapons, opposing the opinion of Demochares and the silence of Thucydides with respect to the testimony of Plato and Antisthenes, he says: "The Cynic is pleased to render homage to Socrates at every opportunity." It is in this way that, wishing to undermine Antisthenes' authority, he makes us understand what the ancients thought of his lively and pious affection for his master.

In Antisthenes' works, then, the Socratic influence is preponderant, just as it was in his life, as it was in his doctrine.

Σάθων [Sathon], directed against Plato, marks the relationship he had with the leader of the Academic school or, to put it another way, the fundamental opposition that existed between the two schools from the beginning.

Finally, a letter addressed to Aristippus has been preserved for us, under his name; but Diogenes Laërtius does not mention any letter by Antisthenes; and the agreement of all critics to reject it with other Socratic letters and to attribute it to some rhetor makes it impermissible to be considered as authentic.[10]

Such was Antisthenes' life and such were his writings: the list of his works by the variety of topics that he treated, the development of his mind by the great influences that he absorbed or that he fought against, – do they not merit that we take for an object of study the doctrine that he professed?

---

[10]Original footnote: A response by Aristippus to a statement made by Diogenes (Laërt., II, 68) seems to have provided the subject of this letter attributed to Antisthenes and of a letter that bears Aristippus' name.

Part II:
Antisthenes' Doctrine

Chapter 3: Introduction to Antisthenes' Doctrine

The philosophical ideas of Antisthenes are all concerned with three main points: he had focused his attention on human intelligence and language, he had expressed several opinions on the nature of beings, and the questions he had raised about [man's] conduct in life became the principle object of his inquiries. That division of philosophy into logic, physics, and ethics was not put forward, it is true, until the century that followed Antisthenes; but it naturally lends itself to the mind when his doctrines are studied or even when one examines the list of his works.

His physics hold no great importance; but his logic and his ethics are quite worthy of fixing the attention of the historian of philosophy. No extensive and developed expositions have as yet been given of it; we will try to fill that gap, by collecting all the fragments and scattered testimonies found in ancient writers, by comparing all those texts so as to interpret them individually and holistically.

But it is not enough to consider Antisthenes' opinions in and of themselves; we must identify their true character by comparing them to those of other Cynics; it is important in effect to distinguish that primitive doctrine, which is called Antisthenism, from innovations and exaggerations due to Diogenes and his successors.

When we know the thought of the master finally, and the consequences that it had on his school, all that remains for us will be to appreciate Cynic philosophy. From a historical point of view, we will examine what had an influence on Antisthenes, in what his originality lies, and what actions he exercised on the fate of philosophy. From the dogmatic point of view, we will attempt to determine the merit of his doctrine, to distinguish whatever it possessed of the exaggerated or false, and what it contained of the true, to explain at one and the same time the unfortunate aberrations of the Cynic school and its incontestable greatness.

Chapter 4: Antisthenes' Logic

Antisthenes' logic admits as legitimate the direct knowledge of reality; but restricting the mind to the narrow limits of experience and finding fault with every effort to attain general ideas, it assumes a critical and negative character, and it ends up by substituting words for ideas, and the study of language for that of thought. If it does not possess a philosophical grandeur, if it fails to emphasize a happy penetration in the analysis of intellectual activities, at least it is remarkable in its originality; and it is not without interest to study how a student of the Sophists reestablishes an unshakeable foundation of certainty, how a disciple of Socrates rejects general ideas, and how Plato's co-disciple and rival opposes to his theory of ideas a type of nominalism.

Antisthenes systematically rejected all Eleatic and Platonic speculations, and to their arguments, which he pretended not to understand, he opposed, in a biting and sometimes successful way, the testimony of experience.

When a disciple of Parmenides attempts to demonstrate that movement is impossible, Antisthenes gets up and walks. This demonstration by the very deed, this evidence of the act, ἐνάργεια, διὰ τῶν ἔργων ἀπόδειξις, is according to him more convincing than all reasoning, than any dialectic discussion.

He fights against Platonic doctrine in the same way: "Some of the ancient philosophers," the Scholiast of Aristotle said, "did not, in any way, admit of *qualities*, τὰς ποιότητας, and maintained that that which exists is only such or such thing, τὸ ποιόν [the quality]; thus, chatting with Plato one day, Antisthenes said, 'Oh, Plato, I do indeed see a horse, but not the essence of a horse, a man, but not the essence of a man, ἀνθρωπότητα δ' οὐχ ὁρῶ.' And the other responded, 'You have, just like us, eyes that permit you to see a man or a horse; but you do not have what it takes to contemplate essences.'" We read in Ammonius: "Antisthenes said that genres and ideas are pure conceptions, adding, 'I do indeed see a horse, but not the *essence of a horse*.'" Finally the Byzantine [John] Tzetzes finds differences among Plato, Aristotle, and Antisthenes, and writes: "It is said that three different opinions on the nature of ideas have been produced: Antisthenes sustains that they are simple conceptions: 'I do indeed see a man,' he says, 'and even a horse, but I do not see the *essence of a horse*, I do not see the *essence of a man*.'"

The testimonies that we have just collected reveal to us Antisthenes' opinion on the nature of ideas; and it is from this point of view primarily that it is important to consider them and interpret them.

Did he simply mean that ideas, considered by Plato as realities, as the principle of the essence and even the matter of other entities, do not exist outside the mind, and are nothing but the phenomena of thought, conceptions?

In this case, his opinion is confused with that of Aristotle, and people do not understand that the ancients presented it as a special and distinct theory; moreover, he would acknowledge a certain idea of a horse in general, of a man in general, etc., but he denied any idea that is not that of an object directly perceived by the senses.

But let us listen to the Scholiast: "Antisthenes," he says, "did not acknowledge qualities in any way, shape, or form, *ἀνῄρει τὰς ποιότητας τελέως*." These extremely precise Peripatetic expressions explain Antisthenes' thought in such a way as to leave no doubt; he absolutely rejected (*ἁπλῶς*) those qualities that we can assert of different objects, that is, in other words, every general conception, *τὰ γένη, τὰ εἴδη*. The Scholiast adds: "He acknowledged only such or such thing, *τὸ ποιόν*." So we conceive of the subject with its manner of being, the thing with its quality, but not the manner of being and the quality independent of the subject and the thing."

Antisthenes does not merely deny the objective reality of the idea that Plato acknowledged; he rejects all general and rational familiarities, and, substituting a theory of language for the investigations into the nature and origin of ideas, he will concern himself anymore only with words, expression, discourse, *ὄνομα λόγος*.

"Each thought," he said, "has an object with which it is determined in our mind"; and he adds: "The object represented by this idea can only be represented by it alone; of one thing only, it can have but one thought, one expression. Reality and thought correspond precisely; each idea has its object, and each object has its idea. Such is the double principle on which his logic will rest."

Aristotle himself teaches us that, according to Antisthenes, each thing can be designated by only a single expression. "The false thought," he says, "is not actually the thought about nothing; insofar as it is false, it is the thought about nothingness. As for the true thought of a thing, it is *one* if it represents the essence, but it is *multiple* from another point of view, that of representing either the entity in itself or the entity with its divers modifications, [for example] Socrates or Socrates the musician... Each thing can be expressed not only in a manner that is particular to it, but also, and verily, by terms that are appropriate to something else; thus, one says that *eight* is double, which is the property of a *dyad*... It is therefore a simplicity on Antisthenes' part to have thought that a person can express a thing only by terms that are particular to it, and that one merely asserts the same thing about the same thing."

"By these words," says the Scholiast, "Aristotle reproaches Antisthenes for the foolishness of saying that an expression can represent only the single object that it is the proper expression of, misled as he was by the reasoning that a false expression is not actually an expression about nothing. No matter how inexact and improper the expression of a thing might be, that does not mean that it is not the expression of it. But Antisthenes believed that each object is designated by an expression which is proper to it, and that there is only one proper expression for each object;

for the property that would designate such a thing in particular, but which would not belong to the very thing that one asserts, which would be, in reality, completely distinct... For the same object, there is but one single expression, and he who speaks about the same thing can speak about it in only one way."

Thus, for Antisthenes, the error would be the expression about nothingness; the truth is the expression about an object; but, just as each object is itself and has its own proper essence, it is represented by a single and unique expression that is proper to it, τῷ οἰχείῳ λόγῳ ἓν ἐφ᾿ ἑνός, and one cannot pronounce multiple assertions about the same thing, εἷς ὁ λόγος περὶ αὐτοῦ τοῦ πράγματος.

He summarized his entire doctrine on the relationships of thought and expression with the object, when he said: λόγος ἐστὶν ὁ τὸ τί ἦν ἢ ἔστι δηλῶν [the logos is the expression of what an object is or was]. Our mind does not conceive of, and language does not express, anything but the proper nature of each particular thing, τὸ τί ἦν ἢ ἔστι, τὸ ποιόν [what it was or is, the quality], and one must limit oneself to the judgment that, – one and invariable like the essence of the thing, ὁ τὸ τί ἦν ἢ ἔστι δηλῶν, – pronounces it as itself, i.e, the identical judgment.

This strange theory was the consequence of an initial error. Antisthenes suppressed general ideas, and from that moment on he made every judgment impossible in which we express the relationship between the same subject and the diverse qualities or modifications that those general ideas represent. These multiple judgments that Aristotle speaks about, these judgments, whereby we assert of a being something other than what is particular to it, suppose that the mind, gifted with the faculty of abstraction and generalization, should have risen to the conception of common qualities that it will attribute consequently to different individuals. Now, this is precisely what Antisthenes denied: he maintained that we have no other ideas than those that represent beings, realities, individuals, τό ʌοιόν; he suppressed every general idea, τὰς ποιότητας, τὰ γένη, τὰ εἴδη [qualities, kinds, forms]. Consequently, only a single term remains, the being in itself with its proper essence, and a single assertion, that which expresses that a thing is itself. The second term which supposes the synthetic judgment, what had to serve as an attribute even, disappeared, and there is no longer any relationship except the relationship between the thing and the thing itself, no more judgment than the identical judgment.

While Plato locates true reality in an idea, Antisthenes correctly locates it in an individual [thing]; but he does not believe that he has done enough to combat Plato unless he demonstrates that there is no other idea in our mind than that of the individual [thing]. Once the general idea is rejected, every relationship, every logical connection between objects is rejected; nothing remains anymore but isolated individuals, thoughts, particular expressions, and for each individual [thing] one cannot assert anything [about it] other than its very essence; for every expression that is not its particular expression is the particular and proper expression of some other object, and consequently does not even belong to the first.

This doctrine by Antisthenes led him to deny the possibility of contradictions and to reject definitions. We will soon express his opinion on these two important points.

Diogenes Laërtius relates that after Antisthenes had composed a piece of writing on the impossibility of contradiction, Plato asked him how he could have treated a like topic, and showed him that his thesis contradicted itself, in that he undertook to contradict other men in a work wherein he was establishing the impossibility of contradictions. It is in consequence to that discussion, adds the historian, that Antisthenes published *Satho*, and from that moment emerged the enmity that separated the two philosophers.

Aristotle, on speaking about this opinion of Antisthenes', correlates it to his veritable principle: "It is a simplicity of Antisthenes'," he says, "to have thought that one cannot express a thing except by the terms alone that are particular to it and that one asserts merely the same thing about the same thing. He went on to say that one cannot contradict and almost even that one cannot be mistaken."

Thus, for Antisthenes, if two people speak truly about the same thing, they will express themselves using the same terms, and consequently there will not be any contradiction. If one expresses himself differently, it is because one does not speak anymore about the same thing; the contradiction is only too apparent; the formal and real contradiction is impossible.

Antisthenes appears to have expressed himself about error in a less precise way than about contradiction. However, the negation of error was the natural consequence of his entire doctrine, and, on the other hand, if he had admitted that some man could really be mistaken, he would have recognized thereby real contradictions among the thoughts of individuals. It is therefore probable that he rejected, at one and the same time, both contradiction and error.

A difficulty presents itself here. This thesis, μὴ εἶναι ἀντιλέγειν [contradiction is impossible], equally maintained by Protagoras and by Antisthenes, did it have the same meaning, was it related to the same doctrine, among the Sophists as among the Cynics?

Diogenes Laërtius did not appear to suspect that there was the least difference between them, in the way that they established and developed their opinion; it is, however, a point on which one must insist.

One can be led in two ways to deny the possibility of contradiction: either to regard the truth as indiscernible from error, all judgment as both true and false at the same time, all proposition as equal to its contrary proposition; or to assert that the mind, determined by the very reality of thinking about things such as they are, cannot conceive of a false idea, cannot be mistaken, cannot assert opposites. To maintain the first thesis, one will seek to establish that everything changes without cease, that nothing is truly itself, that opposites, able to coexist in the same subject, can be indifferently asserted by the mind and with the same probability. In order to establish the second [thesis], it will be necessary to show that each thing is perfectly identical with itself and that it has its own essence which excludes opposites: and consequently that the stability of knowledge will depend on the unity and stability of each entity.

One recognizes Protagoras in the first, and Antisthenes in the second. They both say that contradiction is impossible, but the one because he does not admit of the [existence of] truth, the other because he does not admit of [the existence of] error; the one because he recognizes the same value in two contrary affirmations; the other because he does not recognize anything but one and only one possible expression for each subject. Thus, nothing is more opposed to the opinions of the Sophists than Antisthenes' logic. For the former, error and contradiction are as if the natural state and fatal condition of intelligence: to note them is equally pointless, ridiculous, and impossible. Antisthenes, on the other hand, sees in each thought the faithful image of a reality that corresponds with it; he establishes between the fixed and invariable essence of the object and its thought, the proper discourse that it determines in the mind, a union so intimate that error and contradiction are no longer possible; or, at least, the contradiction, far from being real, is merely apparent; far from being natural and necessary, it is merely a passing inattention. What has been preserved for us on this subject is a remarkable statement that shows quite clearly that instead of condemning the mind to irremediable error, he thought that it was made for truth and that he had faith in its natural correctness. "If a man is of an opposite opin-

ion to us," he said, "we must not reduce him to silence, but convince him and instruct him; for it is not
by showing oneself to be mad that one heals a mad-
man." Let us lead this man to contemplate the same
reality that we are considering, and as a result he will
think and explain himself as we do.

It remains for us to speak of Antisthenes' opinion on
the impossibility of definition.

Socrates had shown the importance of definition; but how to define [something] if one does not investigate generalities, as Socrates did? For Antisthenes, the definition would consist not in associating
something to a type by noting the place that it occu-
pies, but rather in associating the thought that represents it to the thought that is proper to some other object. It would be an enumeration merely of two or
more things compared amongst themselves. It is what
results from this passage by Aristotle:

"This gives us the opportunity to raise the difficulty that the school of Antisthenes posed, as well as
others similarly ignorant. They say that one cannot
define the essence of a thing (for a definition is nothing but a long series of statements); that one can only
state the qualities of an object; that for silver, for example, one cannot say what it is, but that it is analogous to tin."

Thus, the οἰκεῖος λόγος, the particular thought
and the particular statement can alone reveal the
essence of a thing, what it is in itself, τὸ τί ἦν ἢ ἐστι.
The proposition by which one defines λόγος μακρός

[extended discourse] is too complex to represent the object in its simplicity, ἕν ἐφ' ἑνός. Its different terms correspond with different objects, between which one establishes a comparison in order to reveal the qualities of the ones by the qualities of the others. Silver, metal, body are all represented by three particular thoughts, expressed by the three words particular to their character; we conceive of their essences; but to try to define them by saying that silver is a metal, and metal a body, is to engage in an unuseful accumulation and to multiply statements instead of elucidating ideas.

If one cannot define, it is all the more necessary to conceive of the thing in itself, and to arrive at the proper expression, οἰκεῖος λόγος. If the error consists in thinking of one thing and speaking about another, if it is merely a confusion of words, the only rule that one could give for the direction of the mind, – is it not to designate each thing by the terms that are particular to it? Consequently, Antisthenes regarded the choice of expressions, and investigation into the true meaning of words, as the principle of all instruction. For him everything is reduced to the question of language, and one can say that the five books, *On Instruction or Categories*, περὶ παιδείας ἢ ὀνομάτων, encapsulated the entirety of his thought.

Before summarizing and characterizing this part of Antisthenes' philosophy, what remains for us is to examine Plato. Could it be that he had never had in mind the philosopher who maintained in opposition to him the impossibility of contradiction and who attacked his theory of ideas? We do not hesitate to assert that, without naming Antisthenes [directly], he often spoke about him, and often discussed his opinions. Let us gather here the references that his dialogs present to us, with the help of which we will attempt to complete this exposition of Antisthenes' doctrine.

Let us cite, to begin with, this passage from the *Sophist*, wherein Plato maintains that many different assertions can be made about each thing, thus refuting the opinion that dominates the entirety of Antisthenes' logic:

> *On speaking about a man, we apply to him a number of denominations; we designate him by his color, shape, size, vices, virtues; by means of which, as in a thousand other cases, we say not only that he is a man, but also that he is good or such and such other thing and so on and so forth. And in the same way we proceed to other objects that are envisaged, each as a single thing, by attributing to it a number of properties and diverse names... By proceeding in this way, we will regale our young apprentices and our stubborn old ones. The first person to come along will object that it is impossible that many things should be one, and that one thing should be many, and behold men before us who are enchanted to tell you that there is no such thing as a* good *man, but that, on*

*the one hand, a man is a man, while
on the other hand, what is good is
good. On more than one occasion, you
have not, I believe, Theætetus, failed
to encounter men who lend themselves
to such arguments, and often some old
men even who, by their poverty of
mind and knowledge, stand in admiration before these sorts of thing, and
imagine themselves to have found
treasures of wisdom.*

Plato then speaks about those philosophers
who maintain that "nothing has the quality of entering
into communication with any other thing" and [who]
"do not wish to allow that one thing should be called
another." – "They will be obliged," he said, "to examine their own use of language in a most amusing
way... they must necessarily use the words *to be, sep-
arately, the same, other*, and a thousand others of the
same sort, incapable as they are to avoid using them
in their discourses; to the effect that they have no
need of anyone else to refute them, but harbor, as the
saying goes, the enemy in their midst and bring their
own gainsayer along with them wherever they go."

One will recognize here the same theory that
Aristotle and the Scholiast exposed. Antisthenes begins from this principle: that whatever is one [thing]
cannot be multiple [things], and he concludes that
each thing can be designated by one name alone,
ὄνομα. According to him, one thing would be unable
to participate in another: one must not say that a man
is good, but only that a man is a man, in other words

to assert the same thing about the same thing.[11]

The most important reference that Plato made to Antisthenes' doctrine is to be found in *Theætetus*. "It has been asserted," said Socrates, "that the primitive elements, which man and the universe are made of, *cannot be explained in words* (λόγον οὐκ ἔχοι); that each element, taken in itself, cannot be named [individually] (ἕκαστον ὀνομάσαι μόνον), and that it is impossible to say anything more, either for or against it; for that would be to attribute to it being or non-being; that one must not add anything to the element if one wishes to speak about it alone; that one must not even join to it these words, *the, this, that, each, alone*, nor any others like them; because, not having anything fixed about them, they are applied to all things and are always in some way different from those to which they are joined; that one would need to articulate the element in and of itself, if that were even possible, and if there were an explanation that were proper to it (οἰκεῖον λόγον), by means of which one can articulate it without the aid of any other thing; but that it is impossible *to express in words*, any of the primary elements (ἀδύνατον εἶναι ὁτιοῦν τῶν πρώτων ῥηθῆναι λόγῳ), and that one can merely name them simply, because they possess nothing beyond their name (ὄνομα γὰρ μόνον ἔχειν); that, on the contrary, for the things composed of these elements, as there is a combination of these principles, there will also be one of their names that *makes up a discourse (τὰ ὀνόματα αὐτῶν συμπλακέντα λόγον γεγονέναι*); for discourse results essentially from the assemblage of

---

[11]Original footnote: Cratylus also said that there is for each thing a name particular to it and that naturally belongs to it.

names; that, thus, the elements are neither *expressible through discourse*, nor recognizable, but merely sensible (*ἄλογα καὶ ἄγνωστα εἶναι, αἰσθητὰ δέ*), while the composites can be known, articulated, and *become the object of a true opinion*; that, consequently, when one has *formed a true opinion about a thing, but without expressing it in discourse* (*ἄνευ λόγον*), the soul, in truth, was thinking correctly on that object, but did not know it, because a person has no knowledge of a thing so long as he cannot give, or hear, the explanation of it through discourse; but when he joins *his expression through discourse to a true opinion* [of the thing], he is then able to know and possess everything that there is to know [about it]."

In this passage, Plato delves even further into this opinion of Antisthenes' that there is but one single expression for each and every thing; at the same time, he develops it and provides additional details on several points.

In the first place, he distinguishes the simple thing from the composite, and makes us thus understand Antisthenes' thought on the relationship between *ὄνομα* and *λόγος*. If one wishes to designate the simple thing in itself, it can only be done through a single name, *ὄνομα*; but, when diverse elements are brought together to form a complete whole, then the names, brought together amongst themselves, give rise to a *discourse, λόγος*, and the entirety of particular terms designating the elements will form the *particular discourse, οἰκεῖος λόγος,* which will represent the complex whole.

In the second place, words are divided into

two types: the particular word that designates a simple thing; and, on the other hand, words that, having nothing fixed about them (περιτρέχοντα), apply to all things (προσφέρεται, προστίθεται) and which are always different in some way (ἕτερα ὄντα) from the things to which they are joined. And, in effect, as Antisthenes had rejected every general idea, it could no longer remain outside the particular idea of the individual [thing] except in vague and indeterminate terms.

Finally, the simple thing, it is said, is only sensible, αἰσθητά; it gives rise to an opinion, δόξα, but not to a true understanding; for there to be knowledge, there needs to be a developed expression, judgment, discourse; it is, then, the λόγος that constitutes knowledge. To whom to ascribe a like doctrine, if not to Antisthenes? And is it not the natural consequence of all his logic? Above experimental understanding, – that is, above opinion, – he acknowledged only words; the art of thinking well, then, must be conflated for him with the art of speaking well. Everything is reduced to the question of words, and knowledge could not be found except in an exact word and in appropriate language.

That text of the *Sophist* and that remarkable passage from *Theætetus* enlighten us on the great question that dominates all Antisthenes' logic, that of the relationships between the expression and its object. As for that thesis on contradiction and error, Plato made reference to it in his *Euthydemus*.

Euthydemus asserts that one cannot lie, because nobody says what is not; someone who would lie would speak about the thing under question, in other words, of what is; therefore, he would be telling the truth:

In the name of that very principle, [that] nobody says what is not, Dionysodorus proves that two men cannot contradict each other. "Do we contradict each other," he said, "when neither one of us states a thing for what it is, – or is it not more true [to say] that neither one of us is speaking about the thing?... When I say what a thing is and you say something else, do we contradict each other at that time? Or rather, did I speak about this thing here, while you yourself did not speak about it at all? And how is it that someone who does not speak about something could contradict someone else who does?"

"I often hear this proposition put forward," said Socrates then, "and I always admire it. The school of Protagoras and also the most ancient philosophers ordinarily employ it. It has always seemed marvelous to me, and destroys everything and destroys itself. I hope that you will teach me better than another the true reason. One cannot say false things, that is the meaning of the proposition, correct? It necessarily follows that he who speaks, says the truth or says nothing at all... Does one mean by this that it is impossible to say false things, and that it is only possible to think them?" – "No, not even to think them," Dionysodorus replies. Then Socrates, pushing this doctrine to its ultimate consequences, forces the Sophist to admit that neither ignorance nor ignorant people exist, that it is impossible to be mistaken and impossible to make a mistake while acting.

It is quite certain that while writing these pages on error and contradiction, Plato could not forget that the opinions he was combatting found a defender among [some of] Socrates' disciples; and one can assert that while attacking Protagoras he was also aiming at the founder of the Cynic school.[12]

Let us try, on concluding this part of the study of Antisthenes' philosophy, to bring it back to several principal propositions in order to make its unity and order stand out. Antisthenes said:

> *We have no other idea than the experimental idea representing such or such particular object; the perception of sensible things is the only element of knowledge.*
>
> *To each thing corresponds a thought, an expression that is particular to it.*
>
> *What is simple can be designated by name only; otherwise, whatever is one would need to be considered as multiple.*

---

[12]Original footnote: Cratylus also maintained that one cannot speak falsely, because to speak falsely would be to speak about what does not exist (*Crat.*, p 429 b; – trad. by M. Cousin, vol. XI, p. 125); that no names [of things] exist that are more correct than others; that all names are correct, all those at any rate that are names; that if a man seems to speak falsely, he is merely making noise, he is striking the air without purpose like someone who strikes a bronze vase... There is, on this point, something remarkable between the ideas of Antisthenes and those of Heraclitus' disciple.

What is composite can be articulated by a complex expression, through discourse; the entirety of names designating elements will form the particular discourse corresponding to the composite.

In this way, whether it is a matter of the simple or the composite, one can never assert anything about a thing other than the thing itself; the only true judgments are identical judgments; for, outside the name and its proper expression, there are merely terms that have nothing fixed about them, apply to all things, and are always different from those to which they are joined.

One cannot define [anything]; for the definition would consist in asserting about a thing what is distinct in itself.

Contradiction and error are equally impossible; for a person cannot think about and express what does not exist, and, as soon as he thinks about what exists, he can express it in one way only, by the name and through the words that are particular to it.

When a man seems to contradict and to be mistaken [about something], he thinks about one thing, [but] he speaks about another; the error is in his words.

The only rule to follow to arrive at the truth is to investigate the true meaning of words and to articulate each thing in the terms that are appropriate to it.

Knowledge is the discourse that is appropriate to the thing.

The entirety of Antisthenes' logic depends, as already mentioned, on the relationships that have been established between the mind and the object.

According to him, each thing is one and identical to itself, and it determines in the mind, through a direct and immediate action, a thought that is both one and identical, together with a proper expression which alone corresponds to this true thought. The mind, through that intimate union with reality, enters into possession of the truth that the Sophists contested it; and, as Antisthenes does not admit the coexistence of opposites in the same object, and as he is filled with faith in the natural rectitude of the mind, he goes so far as to deny the possibility of contradiction and error.

But, at the same time, he does not wish to admit any other idea in the mind than the specific idea determined by the object, which is to say the particular idea expressed by the name, nor any other judgment than the identical judgment, asserting that the thing is itself.

Apprehensive lest he might leave room for errors, hypotheses, and vain systems, he condemns every effort of the mind in order to rise above empirical knowledge, all active procedures through which the intellect transforms initial ideas and attains general ones. Hence the totally critical and negative character of his logic, the profound difference that separates him from Socrates, and his opposition, in the name of facts, to the arguments of the Eleatics and Plato's theory of ideas.

But to deny general ideas, – is it not tantamount to regarding them as mere words? We find in Antisthenes an error that the Middle Ages made famous, and, if it is permitted to designate a system [of thought] barely suspected until now in the history of Greek philosophy by a recent expression, we will say that his logic is a perfectly-avowed, clearly-formulated, strongly-bound nominalist doctrine, undoubtedly the most precise, consequential, and complete that antiquity presents.

Chapter 5: Antisthenes' Physics

Several works by Antisthenes were related to physics, and it is enough to scan their titles to be certain that his interested was equally divided among the three great objects of that science: God, nature, and man. The ancients do not tell us what he thought about the material world; and his opinions on God and on man are not known to us, neither through the important fragments [left to us] of his work, nor through the somewhat scantily-developed testimonies of his contemporaries; we are therefore reduced to carefully studying, reporting, and commenting on several sparse texts from among later writers. It is what we are going to attempt here.

Antisthenes' teachings and [body of] work contributed to the dissemination of the great truths recently acquired by philosophy through the genius, one could also say through the martyrdom, of Socrates.

Thus, in his treatise περὶ φύσεως [On Nature] he proclaimed the unity of God and pitted that Socratic dogma against the plurality of divinities put forward by diverse nations; recognizing also the spirituality of God, he sustained that our eyes cannot see him, that nothing resembles him, that no image, no material representation, can give us an idea of him.

Antisthenes undoubtedly reproduced many of

his master's ideas on Providence; it is a belief disseminated in his school that a wise man lacks nothing, for
he has the Gods themselves for his friends, and everything is shared between friends. The morality of the
Cynics would seem thusly to be attached to the
knowledge of God and to assume a religious character; but, in general, it has its point of departure and its
goal in man himself; it makes the perfection of our
nature depend on a completely internal principle: effort; and finding a sufficient support in human energy, it does not seek any principle of a more elevated
order for virtue.

Antisthenes did not apply himself to establishing, through new considerations, that belief in the existence, unity, and spirituality of God; he did not even
try in his works to expose the doctrine of his master
in its entirety or to develop it in a scientific manner.
Instead, he borrowed a few isolated principles from
Socrates and presented them as consecrated principles, in the name of which he expected to judge and
combat the religion of his times. Thus, the work περὶ
φύσεως [On Nature] was much less a philosophical
treatise on the existence of God and Providence than
a work directed against polytheism.

Xenophon and Anaxagoras had attempted a
criticism and natural explanation of religious myths.
Socrates doubtless approved of their system of interpretation; but he did not associate himself with it except with extreme reserve. "I feel some apprehen-
sion," he said, "when it has to do with calling a God
by his real name." He did not dissimulate, then, the
difficulty [he had] conciliating the myths of polythe-

ism with the philosophy he succeeded in teaching to the world; but he limited himself to establishing a great doctrine, and he left to others the task of drawing consequences from it and, in this way, combatting traditional errors.

Anaxagoras' exile and the death of Socrates did not inspire prudence and submission in Antisthenes; he freely discussed, and boldly attacked, popular beliefs and religious institutions; he railed against the priests and their promises of future life, he haughtily demonstrates his disdain for the Orphic mysteries and laughs at the vain practices that are supposed to merit for initiates an infinite happiness in the hells. The mendicant priests of Cybele address themselves to him, he responds to them with the worthy words of the celebrated Diodorus: "I do not nurture the mother of the Gods, they take responsibility for doing it themselves."

However, he did not fail to recognize in the mythological traditions a profound meaning that he took pleasure in revealing; they were, for him, the obscure and poetic forms of the wisdom of the first ages, and he tried to discover under the veils of those allegories the philosophical thought that they contained. Clement of Alexandria preserved for us a passage by Antisthenes that clearly shows the character and boldness of his interpretations: "If I could get ahold of Venus, I would pierce her with arrows; for it is she who has debased so many noble and excellent women among us; love is a corruption of our nature, and the unfortunate people whom it takes control of call God the malady that torments them." Similarly,

Antisthenes seems to have attempted a philosophical explanation of the myths related to Bacchus; and for him, Mars, ceding to the counsels of Minerva, was the wise man who, in all his actions, is guided by virtue.

Thus interpreted in the name of philosophy, paganism was no longer a religion, but a collection of fictions and symbols on which the imagination of early man had been fixed. Anymore, his Gods were merely forces of nature or human passions deified by ignorance or madness. Such was the opinion that Antisthenes maintained in his περὶ φύσεως and which he developed in his numerous works on the Homeric poems.

He acknowledged in man a soul superior to the body. His entire moral philosophy demonstrates it, as numerous passages from the ancients establish. The soul, he said, through knowledge and effort, leads us to virtue; from the soul comes all human dignity; to seek the riches that are proper to it, man should improve himself and perfect himself; to neglect them is to lower and degrade himself.

But what is the nature of that soul? What are its faculties? Antisthenes' thought on these questions is unknown, and we do not even know whether he had discussed them.

Finally, what is our destiny? Doubtless, he expressed his opinion on the immortality of the soul in his dialogs: περὶ τοῦ ἀποθανεῖν [On Dying], περὶ ζωῆς καὶ θανάτου [On Life and Death], περὶ τῶν ἐν Ἄδου [On the Afterlife]; but they are completely lost, and no fragment of his works, no testimony by the ancients, provides a satisfactory response to this question.

Antisthenes said, it is true, that the most fortunate thing that can happen to a man is to die content. Death, therefore, in his view, is not a bad thing, and ethical men, far from fearing it, wait for it and desire it. The Cynics think, along with Socrates, that life is a preparation for death. What philosophy, more than Antisthenes', teaches man to purify his soul, rendering it independent of the body, and to detach oneself from life's possessions? This contentment that he speaks of, it is the conscience of having lived well, it is the possession of interior goods, the riches of the soul, it is the assurance of a new and happier life. He also said that anyone who wishes to become immortal must align his entire behavior with piety and justice. The immortality that is promised as a recompense, it is certainly not the reputation or glory that the wise man has learned to scorn; it is the new life that the Gods reserve for the ethical man.

Finally, in his writings on Homer, Antisthenes said that the soul retains in another life the form of the body that it inhabited [in this one]. One must recognize then that he acknowledged an immortality, a future life, at least for those whom their virtue had made worthy of it.

Thus, he contented himself with reproducing the essential ideas of Socrates on the existence and nature of God, on the soul and its immortality. If the ancients

rarely spoke about his opinions on physics, it is because they were not original and he had not even presented them in a fully worked out or scientific manner. They were put forward in his works, rather, as
isolated assertions. It is the same with his physics as
with his ethics, whose character is primarily critical
and negative; if he borrows from Socrates several
great thoughts on God and man, it is not in order to
examine applications of them in real life, but to interpret the myths and criticize traditional religion.

Chapter 6: Antisthenes' Ethics

"The purpose of man is to live in conformance with virtue"; such is the great principle that dominates Antisthenes' entire ethical philosophy: he had established it in one of his most important works, in *Hercules*, and he was content with reproducing it under different forms: "Whatever action the wise man takes," he said, "he is guided *entirely* by virtue, κατὰ πᾶσαν ἀρετήν; the duties that it imposes on him must be more sacred to him than encoded laws."

But was it enough for him, from the beginning, to have pronounced that beautiful name of virtue and then to have repeated it without end? Must we not ask him what the good is, whence our knowledge of duty comes, and in the name of what authority he prescribes rules of conduct to us?

On these important questions he kept silent, and his ethics has no more the character of a well-examined and profound knowledge than other parts of his philosophy do. A pupil of Socrates, he contented himself with collecting his master's legacy, and he did not think that there was any need to elucidate those great ethical ideas with which such a master's conversations had familiarized his mind: virtue, goodness, duty were accepted and consecrated expressions for him; besides, how would he have defined them, he who considered every definition as impossible? If it is true that one can only assert the same thing about the same thing, one must limit himself to saying that virtue is virtue, good is good, etc.[13]

But if he does not wish to define, it is because, as we have already shown, he is reluctant to introduce diversity and modification into the essence of each thing; and, in particular, if he refuses to explain, by other ideas, the idea of what the good is, it is better to note that the good is perfectly one and identical with itself.[14]

While Protagoras recognizes particular virtues that can oppose each other and destroy each other, Antisthenes maintains that virtue cannot be different from itself, that its essence is one, and that the conditions in which we find ourselves do not introduce any diversity into it. "Virtue," he said, "is the same for man as for woman." He recognizes, on the other hand, that the distinction of good and evil does not depend on vain opinions, that the essence of virtue is absolute and immutable; thus, when the Athenians be-

---

[13]Original footnote: Plato is clearly referring to Antisthenes when he speaks of those philosophers who make the good consist in the intelligence, but who cannot explain what the intelligence is, and who are reduced to saying that it is related to the good. "And how would it not be amusing on their part to reproach us for our ignorance with respect to the good and to speak to us then as if we knew it? They say that it is the intelligence of the good, as if we were supposed to understand them from the moment they pronounced the word good." *De rep.*, VI, p. 505 b. – Trad. de M. Cousin, vol. X, p. 48.

[14]Original footnote: Xenophon ascribes to him these words, which show that in essence virtue has no opposition, no possible contradiction: "The excellence of justice is incontestable; sometimes valor and wisdom seem harmful to our friends, but justice never contains any admixture of injustice." Xenophon, *Symposium*. IV, [pp] 38 and 39.

grudgingly heard that verse by Euripides, which seems to have inspired the Sophists – "Is an act shameful when it does not appear as such to the person who performs it?" – Antisthenes said, "Evil is always evil, whether it appears so or not."

Like Socrates, he identified the good with the beautiful: "What is good," he said, "is also beautiful, what is bad is ugly." But he was content to articulate this principle without explaining it and without augmenting it with the dialectical investigations by which Socrates had arrived at it. Later we will see how it was interpreted by his successors, and how these same statements which expressed one of the loftiest conceptions of Platonic metaphysics served to legitimize the most shameful excesses of Cynicism.

These opinions on the nature of the good were not established or legitimized by Antisthenes through an in-depth discussion; rather, by asserting the principle of the unity of virtue and of the immutability of the good, he had assured a stable and unshakeable foundation for his ethical philosophy.

The purpose of his ethical philosophy is to develop men in virtue. "Virtue is learnt," he said, in agreement with Socrates. Thus, this most precious good, the only true one, does not depend, like others, on the chance of our birth or the capriciousness of fortune; it is not the privilege of some favored beings; everyone can attain it.

But how is virtue learnt? How is man formed in the practice of the good?

By reflection, Antisthenes replied, but primarily by struggle and effort.

He applied himself to showing that, in order to become virtuous, man must cultivate his body by gymnastic exercises; that we must above all develop in ourselves a correct judgment and sane reason, *νοῦς*, and the qualities of prudence and wisdom, *φρόνησις*, which decide our behavior. "Prudence," he added, "is of all ramparts the surest, it is the only one that protects against betrayal; [even] if the walls of a city resist attack, they can be betrayed by a traitor from within, but those [ramparts] of the soul remain unshakable; let us be assured then of the convictions that should be an inexpugnable rampart for us." Interrogated on what he had gained by studying philosophy, he said: "It is knowing how to converse with myself." He recognized, then, with Socrates, that it was useful to observe oneself, to interrogate oneself, and that this perpetual reflection on oneself is an essential condition of wisdom. At the same time, he wanted those who desire to make progress in virtue to instruct themselves by men capable of enlightening them: Someone asked him how to become good and honest: "Listen to those who know," he responded, "and learn from them to correct what is bad in you. The most necessary study is to unlearn the bad."

Let no one, therefore, accuse Antisthenes of having recommended and practiced an unintelligible virtue that is without dignity. The words that we have just cited, his so numerous and varied works, the teachings and counsels that he loved to dispense, ev-

erything testifies that, for him, a cultivated intelligence, *νοῦς*, well-reasoned convictions, *λογισμοί*, and
clarified knowledge of the good, *φρόνησις*, are an indispensable preparation for virtue.

But, at the same time that he was seeking to develop
good sense, judgment, sane reason, to shed light on
practical truths, he regarded as useless, even harmful,
subtle and arduous knowledges, vain speculations that
have no relation to virtue, which is our supreme goal.
Virtue, he said, is in action, and it does not require
many words nor great knowledge. Indeed, in order to
raise morality to a level that the Sophists' art could
not attain, he will show that true worth is not speaking well, but doing well, that in order to arrive at
virtue it is not enough to be instructed and to reflect,
but that the perfection of ourselves is at the price of
constant effort and painful struggle.

"Work is a good," or rather: "Toil is the good
par excellence, ὁ πόνος ἀγαθόν." Such is the famous
thesis put forward by Antisthenes in *Cyrus* and in
Hercules. While another disciple of Socrates confuses
the good with pleasure, he undertakes to prove that
the true good is in work, in toil. It is through exercise,
he says, through effort, privations, suffering, through
ἄσκησις and *πόνος* that the soul will diminish the
needs of the body and constrain it to obey it, that it
will acquire those eminent qualities of the sage: firmness, constancy, which Hercules and Socrates gave
such glorious examples of: *τὸ καρτερικὸν, ἀνδρεία,
ἰσχύς*.

The life of Antisthenes is nothing but one beautiful and vast application of his doctrine: placed by birth in the most humble condition, he had loved it because obscurity, he said, is a good and it has the same advantages as work and toil. Each day he comes from Piraeus to Athens in order to hear Socrates whose male virtues he imitates; he proposes Hercules for a model and merits comparison with him; he is content with the coarsest of nourishment, and no other clothes than a mantle folded over his shoulder; hard on himself, he has the right to be hard on others and treats his disciples severely; if he takes special notice of Diogenes among the others, it is because he recognizes in him a friend of toil.

In the same way as he had identified toil as a good, he identified pleasure as bad: "Better is madness," he exclaimed, "than voluptuousness; may I become mad rather than abandon myself to pleasure. The pleasures of the senses, he said to his friends, do not merit the lifting of a finger; anyone who abandons himself to pleasure condemns himself to deceptions, regrets, suffering, the cruel expiation of extremely weak and extremely fugitive sensual delights."[15] When someone boasted to him about the delights of a voluptuous life, he retorted: "I wish them only upon the children of my enemies"; and he considered love like a malady of

---

[15] Original footnote: "Pleasures that do not enter through the door," he said, "cannot leave through the door; we are reduced to excising them with a knife, treating them with hellebore, or subjecting them to famine; and, through a cruel retribution, we will sadly make amends for some weak and fleeting pleasures." Stobæ., t. VI, 2, *Gaisf.*, p. 182...

the soul, like a corruption of our nature.

That proud contempt for pleasure, that fight against the passions, that declared war on our sensitive nature, – it is the dominant character and incontestable originality of his moral philosophy and that of the Cynic school. One could say that Stoicism is already right there in its entirety.

But it is not enough to renounce voluptuousness, one must also detach oneself from all those beguiling goods which common people seek out.[16] The desire to possess them is no less powerful than the seductions of pleasure for distracting men from wisdom; and he who aspires to virtue will need to annihilate in his soul the immoderate zeal for the sciences and the arts, the thirst for riches, pride of birth, ambition, a preference for praise, the desire for beauty and adornment, the love even for life.

After having declared that virtue has no need of many words nor great knowledge, Antisthenes added that, in order not to be distracted by external occupations, the man who has arrived at wisdom will renounce even the study of letters. The *beaux arts* did

---

[16]Original footnote: Arrian [of Nicomedia] says that Antisthenes gave Diogenes true freedom by teaching him how to distinguish between what belonged to him and what did not depend on his will, τὰ ἐμὰ καὶ τὰ ἀλλότρια. But nothing authorizes us to acknowledge that Antisthenes ever distinguished real goods from false ones in this way. Between him and Arrian lie all the great minds that have ever honored the Stoa, and the historian attributes to Socrates' disciple thoughts and expressions that are entirely Stoic [in nature]: σὸν οὖν τί; χρῆσις φαντασιῶν. See Epict . Dissert., III , c. 24 , 67 .

not find approval in his eyes; for he taught that the trouble one took to excel in them got in the way of making great progress in virtue, in the same way that a good musician can be nothing more than a rather bad man.

As for fortune, he demonstrated that it was not at all a veritable good; that its value depends on the soul which alone, if it is mistress of itself and moderate in its desires, is always content with what it possesses, but otherwise finds nothing in the world that might satisfy its insatiable avidity.

"I think, oh my friends," said Antisthenes in Xenophon's *Symposium*, "that wealth and poverty do not at all reside in our houses, but in our souls. How many men I see who, possessing immense goods, find themselves so poor that, in order to acquire still more of them, endure every labor and brave every danger. I know brothers even who have inherited equal portions and one possesses what is necessary [to his life], even [what is] superfluous, while the other does not have enough to meet his needs. The thirst for wealth is such a state of affairs with certain kings that they commit crimes which the most deprived mortals would blush for. Indigence, it is true, leads to stealing, but there are kings who, in order to enrich themselves, ruin families, execute thousands of men, and reduce entire cities to slavery. How I pity them for the cruel malady that gnaws away at them! Do they not resemble a man who, seated at a table loaded with dishes of fine food, would always eat without ever getting full?"

Antisthenes expressed the same thoughts more

briefly when he said, "Without friends, the banquet lacks charm, and even wealth would be unable to make us happy without virtue." In effect, if the desire for wealth is not tempered by virtue, it excites in us incessant torments, "and, stirred by envy, we are consumed by our very passion, like iron by rust." Then we are enticed to [commit] all injustices and all crimes; "for he who loves money cannot be a good man, neither on the throne nor in private life." Finally, without virtue, we constantly depend on the capriciousness of fortune and at every instant we fear lest it turn against us and that its gifts, always changing, might pass into the hands of other men; "now, to live with similar fears is to be a slave without knowing it."

We are already familiar with Antisthenes' scorn for the privileges of birth. The only distinction, the only merit that we, as men, ought to ambition, is the perfectionment of ourselves by wisdom: "virtue," he said, "is true nobility."

What does it matter, from then on, what others might think of us, provided that we have nothing to reproach ourselves for. We ourselves are the true judge of our actions, and the good testimony of our conscience makes our dignity answerable to it alone. The judgments of men lead astray and their praise is addressed to those who least deserve it; "this is why Hercules recommended to his children not to have any obligation to those who praised them, in other words not to accept their praise with blushing and not to respond by flattery." "If someone said to Antisthenes that many people praised him, he responded, 'have I committed some bad act?'" In the same way, he wished people to pay little attention to slander and insults; "for he who slanders casts stones at himself, and is it not the privilege of kings to hear insults on account of the good that they have done?"

The wise man does not merely scorn the empty words of other men; he knows that in order to obtain their approval, he would need to imitate their conduct, and therefore he rejoices in being blamed by them, and he is proud to provoke their criticisms and their ridicule.

But above all he fears their flattery; for nothing is more suited to seducing and corrupting a good man, and if we are wicked, it makes us even worse. "Courtesans," said Antisthenes, desire all sorts of qualities and possessions in their lovers, except reason and wisdom; it is the same with flatterers, with respect to those to whom they are attached"; and, by a play on words that is lost in translation, he added: "Better would it be to become the prey of crows, κόρακες, than the prey of flatterers, κόλακες; for the former devour only cadavers, but the latter attack the soul itself."

We ought also to disdain beauty; honestly, how can someone be proud of an advantage that is shared with inanimate beings?[17] As far as adornment is concerned, as far as pointless adjustments and tweaks [to our person], – that mantle thrown over the left shoulder, the only piece of clothing for every sea-

---

[17]Original footnote: According to Diogenes Laërtius (VI, 10), each time Antisthenes encountered a richly-adorned woman he went to tell her husband about the dangers his honor was running. A like tale has little verisimilitude.

son, [is] a testimony of the little care that Antisthenes paid to his person; and, if one must believe his biographer, he found fault with those who paid attention to adornment as a sign of the corruption of their morals.

Let the wise man scorn, then, everything that attracts attention to us, everything that flatters our vanity. The most modest condition, the humblest, is that wherein virtue is most easily acquired. "Obscurity," said Antisthenes, "is a good; pomp and pride distance us from the goal."

To detach oneself from all these "goods" is, according to the beautiful expression by Socrates, to prepare oneself for death; he who has renounced little by little everything that makes, in the eyes of the vulgar, the charm of life, will be filled with resignation and calmness during his last moments. Someone asked Antisthenes what the happiest thing for man was: it is, he replied, "to die content." Thus, far from looking upon death as a bad thing, the wise man greets it with joy, and the strength of the joy that sustained him amidst life's battles does not abandon him when they are over.[18]

---

[18]Original footnote: But, through culpable error, will he dare to advance the moment [of death] assigned by the Gods? No; it is to be believed that Socrates' disciple did not encourage anyone to lift an impious hand against himself. An obscure expression, added by Athenaeus (IV, p. 157b) to the pleasantries of the courtesan Nicion, and the text: δεῖ κτᾱσθαι νοῦν ῇ βρόχον, would be unable to prove that Antisthenes had authorized that attempt on ourselves, and a story that I reported about his death could serve to establish just the opposite. I will add that Diogenes did not encourage suicide either: there is something of a proof of it in Diogenes Laërtius (VI, 55), Stobée (sermon 118) who reports the same expression, and a recitation by Élien (X, c. 11) that can be

When reflection, but primarily exercise and toil, will have developed courage, firmness [of character], constancy [in the soul], they will have led a man to scorn pleasure and all the fugitive and deceiving "goods"; it is at that time that we will have arrived at virtue.

Now, virtue is our ultimate goal, it is our sovereign good; that is why, he who has acquired it once will be unable to lose it and has nothing more to desire.

Virtue, said Antisthenes, is a weapon that no one can steal from us. It holds the first rank among those provisions that the wise man has assembled and that, even during a shipwreck, he always carries with him; protected by the strength of the soul and reasoned convictions, it remains sheltered from all attempts on it, and does not depend on external things. But the wise man, can he be deprived of it through his own fault? It is probable that Antisthenes acknowledged in an absolute manner that virtue could not be lost and that the wise man is infallible; this opinion in fact was strongly shared by Socratic philosophers; Diogenes Laërtius says that it was common to the entire Cynic school, and if Antisthenes had not accepted it, he would not have permitted to the wise man, – as we will see him do in a moment, – the use of pleasures, and possessions that would turn any other man away from virtue.

---

used against the story about Antisthenes; one must also point out the silence of the Pseudo-Diogenes and the Pseudo-Crates who would not have failed to mention suicide if it had been a point of honor in the Cynic school.

He thought also that the wise man no longer has anything to desire: it is for this reason that Xenophon, in the *Symposium*, ascribes these words to him:

> *What I possess is so considerable that I have difficulty myself in accounting for it; seeking only what is necessary, I always find more than enough... let someone take from me what I have, the most miserable occupation would always suffice to provide for my needs. Simple in my life, moderate in my desires, I never wish for what belongs to my fellows... Can anyone possess anything sweeter than that freedom and leisure that permit me at every instant to see and hear what is the most worthy thing to be seen and heard; and, by a favor that I appreciate all the value of, to spend my entire days with Socrates... Add to that, finally, that such riches fill a man with generosity. Socrates, to whom I owe everything that I possess, never calculated with me or weighed against me; he gave me everything that I could carry away. Like him now, far from hiding my opulence, I am pleased to display it before the eyes of my friends; I share the riches of my soul with those who desire it."*

But let us interrogate Antisthenes himself.

Virtue, he said, is the true nobility; it is the source of internal peace and the perfect tranquility of the soul: for it is nothing that might surprise the wise man and seem extraordinary to him, while other men, always stirred by covetousness and fear, always dependent on their fellows or the blows of fate, are slaves without knowing it; he alone is free and independent; it is in himself that he finds his own felicity.[19] Virtue suffices for happiness; it has no need of other help than Socrates' strength of soul.

The wise man in his relationship with other men will be, as Xenophon says, full of generosity and liberality. It is for this reason that Antisthenes willingly gives warnings and counsels, and finds himself happy communicating to others that wisdom and that felicity that he owes to Socrates; like a doctor full of zeal and devotion, he does not even wait for someone to come and request his help, and as soon as he believes them to be useful, he hastens to offer them; but far from setting an example of that inconsiderate zeal and that brutal freedom that his disciples were later accused of, he strikes the right balance and recommends discretion and circumspection to others.[20]

---

[19]Original footnote: The wise man is sufficient unto himself, for everything that belongs to other men belongs to him: αὐτάρκη εἶναι τόν σοφόν πάντα γὰρ αὐτοῦ εἶναι τὰ τῶν ἄλλων. Laërt., VI, 11; for the interpretation of this thought, see the chapter on the other Cynics.

[20]Original footnote: He instructed others not to give their counsels out of context and without discernment: do not forget, he added, that it is too difficult to uproot and transplant old trees. Anton. Meliss., sermon 61. *De malis et improbis. μὴ νουθέτει γέροντα ἁμαρτάνοντα δένδρον γὰρ παλαιὸν μεταφυτεῦσαι δύσκολόν ἐστι.*

The wise man will attach himself particularly to those who merit being loved; for he knows how to discern those who are the most worthy. But who then is the most worthy of love than the wise man himself? All virtuous men are united by bonds of a common friendship; between them will form, by the rapport of sentiments and tastes, a tight and indissoluble society, which Antisthenes demonstrated the advantages of, and celebrated the charms of.

"We must," he said, "hold a just man in higher esteem than a [mere] family relative. In order to become a good man, one must have either ardent enemies or sincere friends; the former turn us away from evil by the severity of their criticisms, the latter lead us to what is good by the sincerity of their counsels. In the midst of life's battles, let us take for allies those who have courage and justice; for it is better to fight with a small number of good people against all the bad, than to fight with a multitude of bad people against a small number of virtuous men. May wise men come together then, one and all, like brothers; the society of brothers who are united is more sure than all fortresses." Beautiful words from someone who, in Socrates' presence, had learnt, by the sweetest of experiences, that the friendship of a virtuous man, and because of him, means having become a *good panderer*, having excelled at bringing together men who could help each other to become better.

Such are, then, the goods that the virtuous man possesses; it is the true nobility, it is the tranquility of the independent soul, it is the perfect happiness, it is, finally, the friendship with men who are like him. And all these examples, and all this happiness, like the virtue that is at the center of it, reside in the depths of his soul in inviolable sanctuary.

But there is more, thanks to virtue: all the other goods will become excellent for the wise man, and he will be able to experience all pleasures.

The rigor of certain formulaic expressions seemed to wrap all the exterior "goods" in a common reprobation and identify them with the bad; but they had only for their goal to show that too much attachment for these possessions turns us away from virtue and consequently from true happiness. For the man who becomes wise, their possession is without danger from then on; he does nothing to seek them out, but he does not believe any longer the need to reject them; virtue, which instructs him to make a legitimate use of them, imparts to them an entirely new value.

Riches, said Antisthenes, has no value or worth without virtue; and, similarly, in his eyes, other possessions are good or bad according to the usage one puts them to; they have no absolute value in and of themselves; they are indifferent things. What is important is the disposition of our minds with respect to them; it is that empire over us and that detachment from all things which ensures that we are not troubled by desire to acquire them, nor by chagrin for having lost them.

Similarly, not finding expressions energetic enough to wither the man who abandons himself to the pleasure of the senses, Antisthenes prefers folly to a similar degradation of his being, and he goes so far as to identify evil with pleasure. When it comes to the man who aspires to virtue, he shows him how voluptuousness is a danger and a redoubtable seduction. But he who has arrived at wisdom has fought against pleasure enough to know that he has nothing more to fear. The good consists in possessing virtue, the bad in being deprived of it; self-indulgence, the weakness that makes us vulnerable to all our passions and fills our soul with agitation and disquietude, that is what is bad; for that is what lacks virtue. But for the man who has arrived at full control of himself, wisdom puts him out of danger of all attempts [on his virtue], and he enjoys pleasure with impunity.

Such is Antisthenes' thought; he has not, then, enclosed the wise man within the walls of an absolute insensibility, and it is to be believed that he never employed the word ἀπάθεια [apatheia]. The following beautiful thought of his has been preserved for us: "One must seek out the pleasure that follows upon toil, and not what condemns us to toil." He recognized, then, that the wise man has the right to enjoy all the pleasures that do not leave a mark on his virtue and which do not leave any regret after them.[21]

But what are those pleasures? Does it have only to do with pure joy, without admixture, which the possession of virtue, the cultivation of letters, and

---

[21]Original footnote: Athen., XII, p. 513 a. Ἀντισθένης τὴν ἡδονὴν ἀγαθὸν εἶναι φάσκων προσέθηκε τὴν ἀμεταμέλητον. One would willingly associate that thought with Epicurus rather than Antisthenes; and of course Athenaeus expresses rather inexactly the thought of the Cynic, who must have said only this: "If some pleasure is a good, it is only that which does not leave a regret."

friendship give? No. Antisthenes permits the wise man all the pleasures equally; and why forbid him the pleasures of the senses, if they pose no danger to him? Provided that his firmness of soul never belies him, provided he always feels the master of himself, his behavior matters little; and, if he is prudent and moderate enough not to create neither pain nor regret for himself, all his actions are without consequence.

Strange inconsequence of a doctrine that at first proscribes voluptuousness with so much scorn and horror and then authorizes all its disorders! Strange contrast between Antisthenes' rigid principles and the freedoms of his behavior!

We had at first investigated how virtue is learnt, how the wise man is formed; we have just considered what the wise man is in and of himself, what the qualities are that distinguish him from other men, what the true possessions are that he owes to virtue, what his conduct is like. Such is the complete exposition of the moral doctrine of Antisthenes.

The condition that he was born into exercised the greatest influence on Antisthenes' entire philosophy; if that influence is felt in his morality, it determines the special character of his political and social opinions in an even more direct way.

Of course, one cannot expect that the νόθος should esteem and vaunt the rights and privileges that a pitiless legislation forever deprived him of. He mocks the pride that gives to Athenians their title of indigenous people; opposes to the nobility of birth a

purer nobility, one of virtue; to that freedom that a
citizen is proud of, a true freedom, that is, the independent possession of ourselves. He frees man from
all submission and all respect for institutions and
laws, and he destroys the ancient city-state spirit
while recognizing and consecrating the sovereign authority of moral law. "The wise man," he says, "ad-
ministers according to the laws of virtue, not according to written laws." He does nothing to inspire in
others a taste for the active life, and when someone
asks him to what point one ought to get involved in
public affairs: "Similarly to how one approaches
fire," he replied: "too far away, and you will be cold;
too close, and you will get burned."

He finds pleasure in showing how far beneath
a wise man's dignity are the natural vices and disorders of statecraft to make him take part in their administration. Tyrants seem more barbarous to him
than executioners even; for the latter strike a man
who has committed an injustice, but tyrants [strike]
someone who remains irreproachable. And, undoubtedly, in his eyes the most violent, the most redoubtable, of all tyrannies is the insensate power of
the people who put Socrates to death, the justest man
among men. "One takes great care," he says, "to separate the rye from the wheat, and to chase loafers from
the army, but one does nothing to separate vicious
men from society"; and he adds that "the states have
lost when we can no longer distinguish between the
bad and the good." Thus does he identify the true
cause of the decadence and ruin of republican states;
they cannot subsist without virtue. At the same time
as he explains the errors, and signals the dangers, of

Athenian democracy, he attacks the very institution on which it rests, by which I mean universal suffrage; he counsels Athenians to decree that asses are horses; and, as this is found to be absurd, he says: "You choose for generals of the people those who know nothing and have no other title than that of the election."

He seems [to want] to suppress private property when he says that everything that belongs to other men also belongs to the wise man; and it is difficult to reconcile the respect for others' goods with that unlimited right which is the privilege of virtue.

In the same way that he attacks the spirit of the city-state, he willingly sacrifices every family spirit: "One must needs," he says, "favor a virtuous person over a family relative." Thus, the zeal and love of virtue which is dominant in the soul of the wise man tend to free him from all civil ties and all blood ties; and his reason, which raises him above the prejudices and the duties of a citizen, also puts him above feelings and domestic obligations.

Antisthenes says, it is true, that the wise man marries in order to have children; but, at the same time, while turning marriage into ridicule, he seeks to dissuade those who ask his advice about it.

Virtue, he says, is the same for women as for men; now, one must recognize that this virtue will free women of those feelings of reserve and pudor that Antisthenes seems to regard as a prejudice and a weakness, and it will teach them to consider their engagements and duties like empty conventions. If Antisthenes blames adultery, it is only because of the dangers it exposes a person to, but he does not forbid the wise man at all from passing unions which his penchants excuse and which a mutual consent authorize.

Thus, while other men seek the rules of their conduct from without, and obey the laws and customs, the wise man, freed from all affection for his fatherland and his relatives, from all duty towards the state and family, free from those bounds which, according to him, the hazards of birth and human conventions impose on other men, is directed only by his virtue and enjoys unrestrained freedom.

The desire to establish and consecrate the absolute independence of a wise man dominates this entire part of Antisthenes' doctrine; the works that were related to it had an especially critical character, and we must be careful not to ascribe to him fixed theories or a positive system with respect to political institutions and social organization.

Chapter 7: Comparison of Antisthenes' Doctrine with that of Diogenes and the Other Cynics

We have just exposed all the philosophical opinions of Antisthenes in their entirety, that is to say, all the early doctrine of the Cynic school, and our task may appear to be accomplished.

But to fully understand and fully appreciate Antisthenes' doctrine, one must investigate how it was accepted and interpreted, how it was developed and modified by his successors. If the Cynic school was perfectly one, if the thought of its master had been faithfully reproduced by his disciples, such a rapprochement would not be very useful; in this case it is indispensable.

The history of Cynic philosophy presents three quite distinct epochs.

The first, during which it was founded and constituted, finishes with Antisthenes' death.

The second, marked by changes and reforms, famous for its exaggerations, begins with Diogenes of Sinope, whose disciple, Crates the Theban, was himself the master of Zeno the Stoic. It ends with the beginning of Stoicism which, while appropriating and tempering the great principles of Cynic philosophy, seems to have made it impossible from then on.

However, certain minds reproach Stoicism for too great a preference for knowledge, too much weakness in conduct; ignorant and bizarre, coarse and violent, they protest against the new school while perpetuating the Cynic tradition, seeking to imitate and surpass Diogenes. If they include in their ranks one Demetrius, one Demonax, one Œnomaus, the majority resemble the wise man only externally, and they only carry the stick, the satchel, the mantle, and wear the long beard in order to dissimulate or authorize shameful disorders and licentiousness. Writers about Greece and Rome cannot mention them without astonishment and contempt. Lucien unmasks them and paints them with such true strokes and in such vivid colors that the portraits he has left of them will never die. Finally, when Christianity dominates in the Roman world, the fathers of the Church shows us the extravagance, the depravation, and the proud vice that still takes shelter under the banner of Cynicism.

This third epoch of Cynic philosophy only ends in the fifth century of our era; it had lasted for nearly eight centuries. If it holds only mediocre interest, that is not the case with the second epoch which is worthy of every philosophical attention. In fact, Diogenes, that mind whose originality cannot be denied, exaggerated and altered quite a few points of Antisthenes' doctrine; one must investigate what Antisthenes became after having been transformed by Diogenes; on the other hand, Crates was the master of the famous man who founded the school of Stoicism; we must investigate the Diogenism taught by Crates to Zeno.

I will explore, then, a summary of the new Cynics' doctrine, primarily that of Diogenes [of Sinope], for it is important to distinguish between the work of the disciple and that of Antisthenes. I will often have to cite Crates who holds so considerable a place beside Diogenes; but I will reference only a few traits from the history of their successors.

I.

Diogenes Laërtius points out the contempt for sciences and the liberal arts as a dominant characteristic of the Cynic school: "They find it good," he said, "to reject everything that is related to logic and physics, in order to attach themselves strictly to ethics... They leave equally to the side the entirety of the sciences... and proscribe geometry, music, and all analogous arts."

These words, true for the Cynics in general, would be unjust if one applied them to Antisthenes: all the while assigning to ethics the first rank among philosophical sciences, he busied himself with physics and primarily logic; his numerous works testify to the cultivation of his mind and to the variety of his knowledge.

When the historian thus characterizes the Cynic school, the memory of the familiar thoughts of Diogenes of Sinope and his famous repartees was too present in his mind: it is Diogenes who contemned as unimportant and pointless – music, geometry, astron-

omy, and other like studies; it is he who, on seeing a
sundial, exclaimed: "and what have we here: a useful
invention for not forgetting when to eat dinner!"
Someone was discussing the celestial phenomena:
"Since when," he said, "did you return from heaven?"
And when he heard speak of music: "With sage maxims," he continued, "one governs entire cities, but
with your tunes and your cadences, could one manage
a single house even?" It is Diogenes who rejects and
who inflicts an absolute condemnation on physics and
logic; and among the works attributed to him and his
disciples, there is not one that can be regarded with
some reason as the expression of a doctrine relative to
nature or intelligence.

All their writings have to deal with morality,
then; but must we regard them as scientific treatises
wherein the strict forms and regularity of exposition
reflected the importance of the subject? No, Cynicism
was never a reflective system, nor a profound philosophy; after Antisthenes, it rapidly degenerated and
became, following the expression of several ancients,
a simple kind of lifestyle.

The new Cynics limited themselves to discussing one or another question of secondary importance,[22] to developing a counsel, to sustaining some

---

[22]Original footnote: The only written works of the new Cynics that
one could consider regular expositions of a moral doctrine are
the treatises by Diogenes entitled τέχνη ἠθικὴ (Laërt., VI, 80),
περὶ ἀρετῆς, and περὶ ἀγαθοῦ, (Sotion based on Laërt., ib.); but
were these actually Diogenes' works? The list by Diogenes
Laërtius is not in accordance with the one by Sotion, which he
himself preserved for us; and he makes an effort to inform us that
Sosicrates [of Rhodes] and Satyre thought that Diogenes had not
written anything at all.

paradoxical thesis; almost all of them wrote letters, and we understand rather well their preference for a genre of composition that allowed them to present their moral ideas in a lively and stimulating manner, but without any connection between them and always according to the spirit of the moment.[23]

The Socratic dialog had given way to witty sayings, lively repartees, mordant revilement.[24] Placed at the bottom rung of society, having nothing to manage, and nothing to spare, Antisthenes, and especially Diogenes, pitilessly attacked vanity, ambition, riches, glory, all the ridiculousness and all the grandeurs; they had, to hear them and to applaud them, an entire people whom that ardent criticism of the opinions and actions of men struck with fear and surprise.

Soon one saw the Cynics imitating in their writings all the witticisms, all the audacities, all the bizarreries of their masters and publishing works that were to attract attention by their very strangeness. A disciple of Diogenes, Monimus, composes in a cheerful style works that hide a serious intent. Menippus has the upper hand on all the other Cynics by the mordant and biting nature of his expressions; he respects nothing, and the most serious subjects are for him [deserving of no more than] a witticism: when he speaks about human life, about that uncertain and

---

[23]Original footnote: Diogenes Laërtius does not mention any letters written by Antisthenes; but he attributes them to Diogenes, Crates, and Menippus.

[24]Original footnote: Diogenes reproached Plato for the length of his discourses... Laërt, VI, 26; cf. Stobæ., serm. 36, *De Garrul.*

ephemeral life, it is in order to subject it to derision; his writings are filled with pleasantries and buffooneries. His compatriot Meleager followed his example and dedicated a work to comparing lentil puree with boiled legumes.

In this way the sad consequences of a contempt for science is noted in the works of the Cynics. But let us be careful not to confuse Antisthenes with similar ignoramuses and like madmen; did he ever by his writings authorize such bizarreries, did he ever debase philosophy and human thought to that degree?

After having collected the testimonies of ancient authors, after having considered the titles and character of works attributed to Diogenes and his successors, we interrogate the Cynics themselves and ask them to give an account of their doctrines.

Several opinions related to logic by Diogenes and Monimus have been preserved for us.

Diogenes, following the example of his master, loved to protest in the name of facts against subtle reasonings, against the temerities of the dialectic; the reserve in which he enclosed himself and the clever pranks that he played on his opponent were not lacking in charm nor philosophical import. Like Antisthenes, he said to Plato: "I do not see the essence of the table, I do not see the essence of the cup"; like him, in order to respond to those who denied movement, he gets up and walks. By a syllogism, someone demonstrates to him that he has horns. "I don't feel them," he said, after having touched his forehead.

"You are not what I am," a dialectician said to him; "I am a man; therefore, you are not one." "If you wanted to speak the truth," Diogenes replied, "you would say that in reality I am a man and that you are not worthy of that name."

These responses by Diogenes are not connected in his mind to opinions on the nature of intelligence, on the origin of our knowledge; he left all the logical doctrine of his master to one side. But the more he scorned scientific research and philosophical discussions, the more he was bound to make use of that critical and negative procedure.

A disciple of Diogenes, Monimus, pushes that extreme defiance of human reason even further and seems to incline towards skepticism. Sextus Empiricus compares him to Metrodorus and Anaxarchus, who represented the tradition of Democritus and Protagoras. Like them, he suppressed every criterium of truth, and with Anaxarchus he compared beings to vain appearances and assimilated them to what presents itself to the mind during sleep and in madness. He considered everything to be empty smoke, in other words he saw no difference between what exists and what does not exist. Marcus Aurelius tells us that, for Monimus, everything was an opinion, ὑπόληψις, and Menander cites the following statement, which he ranks above γνῶθι σεαυτόν [know thyself]:

τὸ γὰρ ὑποληφθὲν τῦφον εἶναι πᾶν ἔφη [he said everything is vanity].

What is more, did no one think that the philosopher who professed not to value the things of

this world would have loved to contest their existence, that he would have combined doubt with moral
indifference from a logical point of view, and that
skepticism would have assisted him in detaching himself from earthly possessions?

That experimental and critical tendency of
Diogenes, that superficial and inconsequential skepticism of Monimus, – it is all there is of logic in the
philosophy of the new Cynics.

In the same way, they had neglected the questions related to nature.

Diogenes claimed, it is said, that through an
exchange of extremely fine particles, all bodies penetrate each other and that consequently everything is
interrelated. He would seem, then, to have accepted
the mechanical physics of Anaxagoras; but Diogenes
Laërtius, who attributes this opinion to him, invali-
dates his own testimony; for he relies on the authority
of the tragedy entitled *Thyeste*, whose authenticity he
recognizes is doubtful.

It is difficult to know what Diogenes'
thoughts were on essence; I would even say on the
existence of God. He often said that the Gods have
given us all that we need, that they are the friends of
the wise man, that thanks to them the wise man is the
master of all things. But is it necessary to understand
those sayings in a Socratic sense and to think that
Diogenes believed in Providence and recommended
that the wise man put his trust in it? Or were they not,
rather, a poetic expression of his admiration for the
power and admirable order of nature? When one

hears him call the senses *Gods*, one is led to admit that, a precursor of the Stoics, he deified everything that in this world has life, power, and perfection: and one would willingly believe that anyone who conformed all his actions to nature, taken as the principle of conduct, admitted nothing that was superior to it and recognized it as the first and absolute principle of all beings.

What one can assert with complete certitude is that by Antisthenes' example the other Cynics showed themselves to be hostile to religion, blaming practices and ceremonies and interpreting traditions in an allegorical sense.

Diogenes ridicules divines, and he regards as vain and deceitful the promises made to initiates; he gives a philosophical explanation of the myths related to Medea and Prometheus: Crates interprets the myth of Vulcan similarly. Faithful to the spirit of the ancient Cynics, Demonax and Œnomaus attack religion, scorn the cult rendered to the Gods, deny divination and the oracles.

All these opinions are, as one may see, of little interest; it is evident however that the new Cynics have never had a fixed doctrine about physics; let us come to ethics which was the real philosophy for them.

II.

In their admiration for Cynic philosophy, the Stoics said this: it is the shortest route for arriving at virtue.

And, in fact, the idea of virtue, – does it not dominate all the doctrine and all the behavior of the Cynics? Their entire school, has it not accepted and applied that great principle proclaimed by Antisthenes: that one must live in conformance with virtue.

But we do not ask Diogenes, we do not ask his successors to explain themselves on the nature of virtue, on the origin of our duties, and to lay down those principles of morality that their master himself had neglected [to establish]. All that we know is that they thought, like him, that virtue is the same for all beings.

They profess also that virtue is learned; but little concerned with re-raising the dignity of the soul by the cultivation of science, they will no longer speak about φρόνησις [practical wisdom]; making all our moral value depend on action and toil alone, they will recognize only a single condition of virtue, exercise, the tension of the soul, the persistence to dominate and to enslave the body. Diogenes says, with his master, that one must have reason or equip himself with a rope, and he speaks of the advantages of instruction; but he hastens to add that the taste for and study of the arts and sciences could distract us from our veritable goal, and that there are other much more important concerns, other much more real and efficacious exercises. Crates, it is true, who by his birth and by his education distinguishes himself from his master and from contemporary Cynics, does not look down on singing the benefits of the muses in verse. But he does not find imitators, and the Cynics continue to repeat that erudition is really quite unhelpful and that books teach nothing.

Virtue, they say, is found in action, and it is from behavior that it must derive all its glory; it is through actions, then, that it must be formed. The road to happiness is long through precepts [alone]; one shortens it through daily works.

Diogenes shows how necessary it is to exercise both the soul and the body; he shows that nothing in life can be done well without exercise, ἄσκησις, γυμνασία [gymnasia, or training], effort, toil, πόνος, and that a sustained application triumphs over everything. He goes even further: he reproaches Socrates and Antisthenes for too much indulgence and weakness in themselves; and, speaking of this internal energy with more force than his master, he creates expressions that Stoicism has since made famous: there is no time to rest, to relax, ἀνεῖναι, and he does not accept interrupting that permanent act of effort, that constant tension, τὸ ἐπιτεῖναι. The toil that he seeks is that which has for a goal, not the good state of the body, but the good state of the soul, εὐψυχία [high spirit]; in other words, its tension, τόνος.

"Pain [or toil] is a good," such is the dominant principle, the supreme idea of all the Cynic [doctrine on] morality; the ancients also often made mention of it, and the Sophists, who wrote letters under the names of Diogenes and Crates, long developed the precepts that are connected with it. They recommend constant and unflagging toil, exercise, fatigue, struggle, effort, tension. If one is not seeking the pain that ameliorates and fortifies, they say, one is soon assailed on all sides by pains that overwhelm us and keep us enslaved; if one must *toil*, it is necessary *to toil*; if one must avoid toil, one must *toil* anyways; for toil alone can keep us from suffering.

Insofar as the new Cynics, through their master's example, identified work and toil as a good, they had, just like him, to proscribe pleasure. Those who have developed the habit of pleasure, Diogenes said, do not renounce it without toil; but he who has formed a contrary habit is happier from a contempt of voluptuousness than from its enjoyment. In fact, seeking out pleasure is to condemn oneself to perpetual agitations, it is to expose oneself to a number of dangers, to a number of sufferings, and nothing is more contrary to that interior peace that is true happiness than such a state. Let us learn to dominate ourselves and to dominate those passions that disturb and trouble our soul; otherwise, we become their slave, and, the more we give them, the more insatiable they are. Diogenes opposes to them then all the strength of his reason, and he boasts about having carried away, of all the victories, the most difficult, by triumphing over anger, desires, fears, and the most dangerous enemy of all: voluptuousness.

Similarly, Crates shows the danger that exists when one abandons oneself to the seductions of love and the disorders of a voluptuous life; and one ascribes to a Cynic of the subsequent centuries these beautiful words: "You add to your virtue what you subtract from your pleasures."

The new Cynics proscribed, in addition to a love for voluptuousness, all the other passions; and on this point their thought seems more firm, more precise than Antisthenes'. Diogenes goes even further than his master when he speaks of an indifference, of an absolute insensibility, and pronounces the word, ἀπάθεια [apathia]. More moderate, Crates investigates merely the strength of the soul and the empire of oneself, ἐγκράτεια [self-restraint]; but there is no doubt that the idea of ἀπάθεια, – which was only in a germ form with Antisthenes and which Diogenes later went on to develop, – had been greatly disseminated among the new Cynics.

All the Cynics oppose, as Antisthenes did, apparent and deceptive goods, real goods, goods conformant with the truth, κατ' ἀλήθνεια. They testify, like him, to their contempt for riches, for praise and flattery, for nobility and that vain rumor that one calls glory; they show how shameful it is to attach oneself to visible beauty by neglecting that of the soul, how the attention given to the body enslaves us and how focusing on personal adornment and ornaments debases us. All these goods, whose possession makes the joy and torment of other men, the wise man regards them as empty smoke, and, breaking free from all the ties that attach us to life, he understands how not to fear death.

But it is not enough, they say, to contemn riches, glory, pleasure, life; one must seek out, one must cherish poverty, an obscure condition, sorrow even. Diogenes delights in repeating that all the imprecations of the tragic heroes have redounded to him; he rejoices in all the trials he undergoes, in all the ills that he suffers; he thanks fortune for giving him such rude lessons. He regards it as a good, that

exile, that poverty that constrains him to do what philosophy seeks to persuade us [to do], and from whose
bosom virtue is born of itself, so to speak.

These same thoughts are familiar to other
Cynics who, desirous above all of freeing themselves
from all servitude, of no longer depending on fortune,
apply themselves to diminishing their needs and making themselves famous by the simplicity of their life
and their severity, by being hard on themselves. Antisthenes had praised virtue; Crates celebrates in his
verses an obscure condition, moderation, frugality,
poverty; he sings the satchel.

But Diogenes and his disciples are not content
with imitating Antisthenes' example and reproducing
his teachings under various forms; it is not enough, in
their opinion, to become detached from all goods,
they demand a complete renunciation; glorifying
[self-]imposed privations and seeking out suffering
with fanatic zeal, they substitute for firmness, for
tranquility of the soul, for the worthy and binding resignation of the disciple of Socrates, a sort of rigorous-
ness and asceticism.

When Diogenes, in order to emulate children and
slaves in their simplicity, rejects his cup and his
spoon, when he takes animals even for models [of be-
havior], when he walks barefoot in every season, rolls
around in the burning sand in summer, throws himself
onto the snow in winter, or embraces all the bronze
statues, there is an intention about him, a bias to out-
do Socrates and Antisthenes. Placed by birth in an el-

evated condition, Crates seems to have received his fortune from the Gods, only to turn around and demonstrate a great and memorable example of abnegation and liberality. He abandons all his property in order to attach himself to Diogenes and to devote himself to philosophy; and, from that day forward, he marks the era of his freedom. "Live in conformance with virtue," said Antisthenes; but to this Socratic principle came to be added a new principle: "Live in conformance with nature," said Diogenes; words that mark a profound change, a transformation in Cynic morality. If one must live in conformance with nature, one must refuse everything that is not necessary to our needs; it is an absolute duty to renounce everything that can be regarded as superfluous, to bring oneself to that state of nature wherein the animals alone present to us the perfect model.

Amidst the rigors exercised on them, the new Cynics paid very little attention to the mind of the wise man and succeeded at no longer considering anything but action, practices, and whatever is external and apparent: "You know nothing," it was said to Diogenes, "but you lay claim to a philosophy." "Even if," he retorted, "I had nothing of the wise man [about me] but external [trappings], that would already be a philosophy." The Cynic wisdom will consist, from then on, in drinking water, eating watercress, begging, insulting passersby, scorning their shamelessness; and, to imitate a beautiful expression by Antisthenes: "Of all weapons, virtue is the surest," one would call the mantle, the satchel, and the stick divine weapons. Thus, to the proud asceticism of the new Cynics a puerile formalism is added; such are the fatal consequences of that conformity of life to nature and of that contempt for reflection and science.

The man who has arrived at virtue possesses the sovereign good; wisdom, once acquired, fills all our desires and can no longer be wrested from us.

Formed by exercise and toil, habituated to the perpetual tension of the soul, the wise man has for dominant qualities energy, male firmness, the patience that resists every test, and unshakeable constancy.

From then on, master of himself, dominating his passions, he lives in the absence of trouble and agitation, in ἀπάθεια; finding in himself all true goods, contemning all the deceiving goods, he is sufficient unto himself; he enjoys αὐτάρκεια [self-sufficiency].

While other men are slaves to their passions, to their attachment to apparent goods, the wise man by ἀπάθεια and αὐτάρκεια arrives at absolute independence. "Freedom is the first of goods," said Diogenes. If Crates renounces his riches and consecrates his life to philosophy, it is in order to free himself and enjoy freedom. Their conduct, like their maxims, testifies to their being dominated at every instant by that need to subtract themselves from the influence of fortune and from other men, and to rely only on themselves; also, the Sophists who wrote under the name of Diogenes and Crates have not neglected that side of the Cynic doctrine, and their letters celebrate at every opportunity the perfect freedom of the wise man.

This ἀπάθεια which keeps the wise man free from fears and deceptions, from all that would trouble the perfect tranquility of his soul, and this αὐτάρκεια which allows him to find in himself all the truly desirable goods, make the wise man perfectly happy. "Misfortune," said Diogenes, "has no other cause than our blindness"; he who possesses wisdom cannot but be happy, and the very scorn of pleasure will be for him a source of infinite joys.

Finally, αὐτάρκεια and ἀπάθεια, while giving to the wise man a perfect independence, a peace of the soul, and an interior calm that nothing can upset, make him an equal of the Gods themselves. "The wise man is in the image of the Gods," said Diogenes. "The Gods," he said on another occasion, "have no need of anything"; the less one has the more one draws near to them.

Thus, their teacher's doctrine is made more precise and exaggerated with the new Cynics.

The idea of αὐτάρκεια was already a part of Antisthenes' doctrine, but ἀπάθεια is not found in it except as the germ of an idea, and, though he had exalted the freedom of the wise man, he had never gone so far as to say that it made him like God himself.

But how will the wise man procure for himself what is necessary for his needs? The response of the new Cynics to this question is inspired by the Pythagorean phrase: "Everything is held in common among friends," and by a vague remembrance of Socrates' teachings on divine Providence. Diogenes often re-

peats that the Gods have put within man's reach all
that he needs to live happy;[25] and, to reassure the wise
man, he shows him quite pertinently that nothing can
be lacking to him; "Everything belongs to the Gods;
the Gods are the friends of the wise man; among
friends, everything is held in common; therefore, everything belongs to the wise man."

From this principle, it followed that everything that belongs to other men belongs also to the
wise man. Such was Antisthenes' thought; but it is
curious to see what development it receives among
the new Cynics. "The wise man," they say, address-
ing themselves to those who have possessions, "does
nothing more than ask for his goods back and repos-
sess what belongs to him": the needs of the wise man
are, in their eyes, like a sort of divine right in the
name of which he appropriates what suits him.[26]
Hence, his proud begging;[27] he thinks he obliges and
honors the man from whom he deigns to take his
share of the goods assigned to humankind by the
Gods; far from showing any gratitude, he demands it,
and he turns away forever from those who do not
show themselves happy to receive him and who are

---

[25]Original footnote: Laërt., VI, 44. – Diogenes added that if we
complain about fortune, it is because we ask the gods for things
that we take to be goods, not real goods: Laërt., VI, 42.

[26]Original footnote: Someone was asking Diogenes to return a
mantle: "If you give it to me," he said, "I will keep it; if you loan it
to me, I will make use of it." Laërt., VI, 62.

[27]Original footnote: Nobody says that Antisthenes begged: his
disciple gave the example. Laërt., VI, 49, 67. – See the
justification for begging by the Pseudo-Diogenes, ep. 5, 240,
Boiss., and the Pseudo-Crates, ep. 3, p. 18, ib. etc.

not willing to have been chosen and distinguished by him.

If we consider the relationship of the wise man with other men, undoubtedly the new Cynics have not forgotten Antisthenes' beautiful words about the affection that unites virtuous men with them. The wise man, they say, is worthy of being loved; and Diogenes adds that a virtuous friend is the best assistance, the most powerful support for the man who exerts himself to arrive at wisdom.

But the wise man reserves his affection for those who resemble him, does not find in his heart any tie that binds him to other men and even shows himself full of contempt and severity for them. Diogenes boasts about knowing how to command men and to being made to serve as their master; he compares them all to children or to slaves and nowhere does he find a man truly worthy of that name. He considers himself like a physician among ill people and in his inquisitive zeal, applying violent remedies to others' woes, he goes everywhere giving counsels with a rude frankness, blaming with bitterness, frightening everyone by his bitter reproaches and his pitiless revilement; he is feared, people run from him when he draws near.

It is no longer the case, as with Socrates, of a man who, led by the love for truth and for the good, by a strong affection for other men, calls them to reflect on themselves, communicates to them a taste for virtue, inspires in them the desire and the strength of acquiring it. If Antisthenes addressed counsels and reprimands [at men], it was still with the moderation and reserve of his master; and then, was he not that *good panderer*, so gifted at bringing other men together in a common love of wisdom? But Diogenes knows no measure, and abandons himself to every verve of his critical and mordant mind: if sometimes he obeys the desire to be useful, more often he is dominated by the feeling of an arrogant superiority.

Crates, *for practice*, would insult courtiers; he entered homes to give advice and was nicknamed the *door opener*. But he appeared more moderate than Diogenes; he was more able to make people listen to him and to make his counsels loved, more desirous to establish and conserve his influence; people turn to him, and, in families, he willingly accepts the role of arbiter and conciliator. After him comes Menippus who turns everything to derision, and whose jokes and perpetual buffooneries are merely vain and sterile witticisms. Is it still necessary to mention that Menedemus who appeared, among the people, disguised as a Fury, and who said he was sent by the infernal Gods to observe the misdeeds of men? We would not cite such extravagances if their authors had not thought themselves excused, if they had not felt themselves authorized, by Diogenes's doctrine and example.

It is through these aggressive habits that the new Cynics sought to justify that name of Dogs which they were so proud of; but they merited it primarily because of their way of life and the strangeness of their behavior.

They are easily pardoned for this bizarre behavior which brings them to walking around barefoot, eating in the public square, sleeping under the porticoes; but they shocked, they revolted [people] by their contempt of any sense of shame, by the public depravity of their licentious lifestyle. One will forgive us for not insisting on the obscenities and the disgusting practices that made Cynicism so sadly famous and that made its name pass into modern tongues by attaching an eternal shame to it.

What is important to us is to understand the principles that provoked and legitimized in the Cynics' eyes the disorders of their behavior.

It is necessary, they said, to live in conformity with nature; everything that is in conformity with nature is good, everything that is good is beautiful; finally, everything that is good and beautiful is as such, independently of the circumstances, in other words, in an absolute manner. In their most astonishing excesses they practiced, they said, in accordance with nature and claimed to obey love by what is naturally beautiful, adding that if a thing is good it must be done in public as well as in private, and if it is bad, it must be done neither in private nor in public. On the other hand, they sustain that virtue is the only good, that nothing is bad except the absence of virtue; they are indifferent to all else. The wise man who possesses virtue is, thanks to it, protected from any attempt [on it]; for, once acquired, it cannot be lost, and whatever our actions might be, it is like the sun whose pure light brightens up all things without anything else subduing its brightness. Finally, the wise man, freed from the opinions and vain prejudices of men, strives to act differently from them and, in testimony of his independence and freedom, braves pudor itself which he looks on as a fake feeling and purely a convention.

Thus the principles that made the greatness of the school of Antisthenes, and soon afterwards the eternal honor of Stoicism, served to legitimize the most shameful aberrations; and the Cynic depravation had for an excuse the absolute immutability of the good, the identity of the good and the beautiful, the conformity of life with nature, the indifference of all things in comparison with virtue which is the only good, the infallibility of the wise man and that freedom itself that makes him the equal of the Gods! That proud philosophy that sought to elevate man above himself and transform him, ultimately let him degrade himself and lower himself to the level of a brute.

The majority of these principles invoked by the new Cynics are, it is true, borrowed from Antisthenes; but the idea of conforming our life to nature belongs to Diogenes; this principle had a decisive influence on his successors and dragged them down an unfortunate path. Let us compare their conduct with that of Antisthenes: without a doubt he allowed to the wise man a great berth in behavior, and he employed an extreme freedom in his own life: but no one had ever accused him of having shocked the eyes, or of ever having offended the pudor, of those around him, or of having outraged their noblest feelings: finally, the *investigation of nature*, as the new Cynics said, led them to habits against nature which Socrates' disciple had never given them the example of. Diogenes and Crates would have surprised Antisthenes; they are primarily culpable for having authorized by their teaching and by their behavior that shameful depravation that made the Cynic philosophy sink below that of Epicurus.

III.

Before summarizing and specifying our thought on the morality of the Cynics, we still have to consider a curious and important side of their doctrine, I want to say their social and political ideas, their opinions on property, family, and the city-state.

The rights accorded to the wise man by the new Cynics include the formal negation and radical destruction of property. Socrates' disciple had said only this: "what belongs to other men belongs also to the wise man," and it was difficult really to fix the meaning and scope of his words: Diogenes' words, however, are perfectly clear and precise. According to him, the needs of the wise man, – his needs conformant with nature and hence even legitimate and sacred, – constitute a right that cannot be taken away from him and that he is free to exert at any time, a sort of divine right in the name of which he comes to claim his portion of the gifts made by the Gods to humankind, to be taken back from the hands of those men who had unduly appropriated superfluous goods.

On this point, Diogenes does not limit himself to reproducing the thought of his master, he develops it, he exaggerates it; and that under a powerful influ-

ence on his mind which made itself felt in all his doctrine: he obeyed his admiration for the institutions and
customs of Lacedaemonia.

On the other hand, the new Cynics sought to
destroy the family. Thus, Diogenes congratulates
those who take the position of not marrying or who
renounce raising their children; and when someone
asked him at what age one should marry, he said:
"young people, not yet; and old people, never." But if
one is to believe his biography, he would not have restricted himself to discouraging others from marriage;
preferring, as he often said, nature to law, he would
have rejected that institution in order to replace it by
the hazards of passing unions based on mutual consent; he would have asked for a community of women
and hence even that of children.

Epictetus in the discourse wherein he praises
the life of the Cynic, and the Pseudo-Diogenes in one
of his letters, limits himself to saying that the wise
man will not marry, will not raise children, lest he
should impose new duties on himself and a thousand
cares that distract him from the cultivation of virtue.
But their silence does not prove that Diogenes Laërtius was mistaken, and it is not impossible on this
score that the opinions of Diogenes recalled the practices of Sparta. It is what one is led to believe when
one thinks of the marriage that Crates reserves for his
son and the revolting procedure in which he marries
his daughter.

Finally, the Cynics, in order to break ties with
the family, taught that people must not have any gratitude for the authors of their days.

Undoubtedly, Diogenes had found in Antisthenes' teaching and examples the germ of opinions that we have just exposed; but let us not forget what Antisthenes said: the wise man marries in order to have children, and that this phrase alone marks a profound difference between the two doctrines.

What were the political ideas of the new Cynics?

Diogenes says, like his master, that one must follow the voice of nature rather than the laws instituted by men, and, by expressing himself in this way, he discounts the state, the city-state, which in his own opinion cannot exist unless there are established and respected laws. Chased out of his fatherland, he learned to despise that idol of antique times; he rejoiced in that exile which led him to philosophy; having become a philosopher, he has nothing anymore of the citizen [about him]: wisdom has killed in him the spirit of the city-state. He engages his disciples not to mix in public affairs. What state is perfect enough that the wise man might deign to take part in its administration? There is but one regular government, the government of the world: the world is the true city-state; and when one asked Diogenes whence he came, he responded with this fine phrase: I am a citizen of the world, κοσμοπολίτης [cosmopolitan].

Similarly, Crates despises all dignities, all honors to which humanity can lift us: apply yourself to philosophy, he said, until you look on the generals of armies as the leaders of donkeys. Little do they matter to him, those cities, those states, the works of our hands, fragile institutions of men; he has not a

single city, not a single roof, for a fatherland; the entire universe is his city, the residence that is prepared
for him. He is hardly concerned whether Thebes, his
birth city, should rise up from its ruins; another
Alexandria would destroy it anew; his true fatherland,
it is obscurity, it is poverty; he is a citizen of Diogenes. The Cynics continued to hold themselves apart
from public affairs, not deigning to busy themselves
with the interests and rivalries of states, while regarding all men as members of the same city-state and the
world as their common residence.

Thus, it was reserved for the Cynics, for those
men who had emerged for the most part from the
humblest of conditions, for those νόθοι, for those pro-
scripts, for those slaves, strongly to conceive of and
to disseminate that great idea of the universal city-
state and of the equality of men. It is probable that
Diogenes and Crates owed it to Antisthenes who,
himself, had gotten it from Socrates' teaching; but
one must recognize that he had the merit of shedding
light on it and on propagating it. The more they had
debased and degraded man by suppressing the family,
the more they elevated him and ennobled him by
erasing the limits of states and proclaiming man a citizen of the world.

IV.

Such was the philosophical doctrine of the Cynic
school after Antisthenes, a doctrine that one could
call Diogenism; for it does not contain any idea that
was not put forward by Diogenes. Crates reproduced

the opinions of his master in a clever way, and they were accepted by all the Cynics of the following epoch.

Let us summarize and go back over several specific points in that long comparison between Antisthenism and Diogenism.

We will not return to [discuss] the relationships that we believe have been made clear by carefully putting together all the ingenious expressions under which the other Cynics presented Antisthenes' thoughts, all the opinions or all the deeds that are nothing but the development or the natural application of his doctrine. Everyone knows that Diogenes was the disciple of Antisthenes, that he accepted the opinions and continued the work of his master, – that is not what is under discussion here. But it is necessary to know on what points, in what measure, and in what spirit Diogenes modified Antisthenes' doctrine, how and why he veered from it; we must enumerate and exactly appreciate the differences that separate them. Antiquity has paid Diogenes a lot of attention; by the singularity of his life, by the strangeness of his opinions, by the vivacity of his repartees, he is in the eyes of the common people the most important person and true representative of the Cynic school. The more famous the disciple, the more necessary it is for us to investigate the traits that distinguish him from his master; our intent is to be honest and just towards the both of them; it is, on the one hand, to more clearly determine the early doctrine of the Cynic school, to recognize the true character of Antisthenes' philosophy and to compare it to the new ideas and to the exaggerations that he would have doubtless disavowed; on the other hand, it is to assign to Diogenes his veritable role, to note his incontestable originality, but also to put the full weight of responsibility of his innovations on him.

The differences between Antisthenes' doctrine and that of Diogenes can be categorized into three main areas: a contempt for science and reflection, the idea of the tension of the soul, the idea of the conformity of life to nature.

Antisthenes, although not having held the sciences in high honor, did not fail to cultivate them, and he had considered reflection, knowledge of oneself, prudence, strong convictions, as important conditions of wisdom. Diogenes goes so far as to cultivate an absolute contempt for the sciences, and regards instruction and reflection as useless for instilling virtue in a man.

Whence, with Diogenes and his successors, the absence of any investigation into physics or logic, the absence of works that embrace ethics in its entirety and treat of it in a complete and regular fashion, the preference given to a light form of the epistle, finally the pleasantries, the buffooneries that fill their writings.

Whence, among Diogenes' successors, the idea that wisdom is independent of the internal state of the soul and consists only in actions, in the external deed, that thought is nothing, that virtue is in practices and external acts; whence that ridiculous formalism that authorized so many ignoramuses and fools to

assume the name of Cynic and which provoked so
many famous extravagancies.

If the new Cynics looked down on the assistance of instruction and reflection, it is because they
believed they found a sufficient support in the extreme energy of their will and the powerful concentration of their efforts. Diogenes reproaches Antisthenes
for too much weakness and self-indulgence, and,
pushing himself much further than his master, he
presents the idea of tension, τόνος; an idea that Antisthenes doubtless would not have approved of, but
which, expressed for the first time by Diogenes,
marks a superior degree of effort and energy in the
disciple.

It is through the tension of the soul, triumphing over all the passions, that he will arrive at that in-
sensitivity, that absolute impassiveness, that ἀπάθεια,
which the disciple of Socrates [Diogenes' master] had
not dared to impose on the wise man.

It is through the tension of the soul that the
wise man, not content with Antisthenes' firmness and
resignation, goes as far as voluntary renunciation,
self-imposed privations and rigors, and he is the first
[person] in Greek society to set an example of asceticism.

It is through tension that he arrives at complete emancipation, perfect liberty; the more the wise
man exercised his will, multiplied his efforts, and
toiled with energy, the more free he feels, and the
more he values that privilege of his virtue. The new
Cynics are, then, more imbued with, and prouder of,

that feeling of their freedom than Antisthenes is; it makes them seem like the Gods themselves, and from that moment forward, deified in their pride, they look at all other men as vile slaves; finally, to give testimony to their perfect independence, they apply themselves to doing the opposite of what others do, and they affect to defy laws, customs, proprieties, and pudor itself.

Antisthenes had taught the conformity of life to virtue, that is, a simple and harsh life, moderation of the desires, contempt of the superfluous, and he had proposed Socrates, Hercules, and Cyrus as examples. But Diogenes is the first to speak about the conformity of life to nature; it is he who presents, as a model of the wise man, the man such as nature made him, the primitive man, child or slave, and finally the animals themselves. In the history of Cynic philosophy this idea belongs to him alone, it has in its doctrine a certain number of great and admirable consequences, but it is also the beginning of new aberrations: simultaneously as it imposes simplicity and severity, it authorizes that revolting behavior to which the name of Cynicism is attached; in the social order, if it leads the wise man to consider all men as members of a great and perfect city-state, which is the world itself, it brings the community of women, children, and goods along with it.

Such are the differences that separate Diogenes' doctrine from that of Antisthenes; but there is one doctrine that dominates all others; it is that of the tension of the soul. That tension leads the wise man to reject, as no longer useful, to scorn as a weakness and a slackening, science, instruction, reflection; it emancipates him from the passions, prejudices, customs, and laws, reduces him to a state of nature, the pupil hence being even greater than Antisthenes and Socrates, and equal to the Gods.

In the same way that Antisthenes had separated himself from Socrates by emphasizing the need for exercise and toil, Diogenes separates himself from Antisthenes by an energy and a stronger concentration, by that tension of the soul. Diogenes exaggerated Antisthenes, just as Antisthenes exaggerated Socrates, and, according to Plato's beautiful expression, Diogenes is a Socrates gone mad.

Chapter 8: Historic and Philosophic Appreciation of Antisthenes' Doctrine

Antisthenes' opinions are far from forming a complete and regular system; he neglected physics, restricted logic within narrow limits, didn't realize the relationships that united these two sciences with ethics; and, on certain points, it is difficult to reconcile the different parts of his doctrine [into a coherent whole]. One might say that he discussed philosophical questions but that he has no philosophy.

If he did not go deeper into questions related to nature and God, it is because he had been particularly struck by Socrates' contempt for the empty hypotheses of physicists and the temerities of the Eleatics. He forgets that his master unceasingly associated human things with the divine, as with their first principle, and that he regarded discussions relative to order and harmony in the world, to the Providence of God, as an essential part of practical philosophy; and, if he asserts with him the existence of a spiritual God, that opinion, detached from the rest of his doctrine, has no influence on his morality which finds its support and its goal in man alone.

One could associate some of the opinions of the philosophers of the same epoch with his logic; but there is no doctrine that, in its entirety, could be compared to his.[28] It in no way resembles the procedures followed by Socrates who, with the assistance of the dialectic and induction, arrived at definition and generalization; it is not the less opposed to the Sophists' opinions.

Perhaps the idea that what does not exist can be neither thought nor expressed is with Antisthenes a recollection of the argumentations by Gorgias; but how far he is, on the most essential points, from that Sophist who claimed that nothing exists; that, moreover, nothing could be known; and that nothing, in any case, could be expressed! Antisthenes admits a real, an incontestable reality, that of the object perceived by the senses, and, for each thing, a thought and a proper expression so exactly corresponding to it that contradiction and error become impossible. Other philosophers will respond to the Sophists in the name of metaphysics and with the aid of the dialectic method; for him, he is content with opposing to them the evidence of the facts, the testimony of common sense, the direct and immediate relationship of the mind with the object that perceives it; he does not leave that narrow circle wherein he has dug in and fortified his position against all attacks by the Skeptics.

---

[28]Original footnote: Thus, Cratylus thought that for each thing there was a name particular to it, that it could not be contradicted, for doing so would be like saying that something did not exist (Plato, *Cratylus*, p. 394, a. and 429, b. – Translated [into French] by M. Cousin, t. XI, 1 and 125); but on other points his ideas differ from those of Antisthenes.

Protagoras, at the core of being as in the mind itself, admits of the possibility of opposites; he asserts that everything is in constant flux, that everything is equally true and false, and hence even that one can neither define, nor be mistaken, nor contradict.

Antisthenes, on the contrary, thinks that each being [or entity] is itself, has a proper and determined essence; he denies the possibility of contradictions in the same subject; if he rejects definition, it is because he believes that its divers elements cannot represent the perfect unity of the individual essence; if he denies error and contradiction, it is because, according to him, each thing can be thought of in only one way, and cannot be represented except by the expression that is particular to it.

Thus, for the one, reality is lost in incessant change, and thought in absolute indifference; for the other, each thing has its proper nature and remains identical to itself, and the human mind, which conceives of it as it is, is in possession of the truth.

To emphasize this opposition, Antisthenes accepts the very expressions used by Protagoras and gives a new meaning to those consecrated formulas: "One cannot contradict, one cannot be mistaken, one cannot define." Of course, in this challenge made to the Sophists, one needs to recognize a singular investigation, something bizarre and sophistical; however, if one looks deeply into it, his logic recalls that of his first teachers, but only through his firm resolution to combat them and his decision to oppose them on every point.

Let us recall, moreover, that Aristotle and the other authors who acquainted us with Antisthenes' opinions do not say that they were accepted by him and borrowed from some anterior system; but they attribute them to him personally and they address their criticisms at him by making him the sole person responsible for them. One must therefore recognize that he had been led to his logic by a personal effort of his mind, and that it would be unjust to contest the merit of originality in this part of his philosophy.

Antisthenes' logic was accepted and presented later by a disciple of Diogenes, Stilpon of Megara. After Euclid, the Megarian school was split into two branches; while Eubulides and his disciples forget life's things and lose themselves in dialectic subtleties, Stilpon teaches and practices Antisthenes' ethics and also accepts his logic; he understands like him the identity of the essence and the immutability of the truth; he thinks that things whose names are different are equally different between them, and that things that are different between them are separated from each other; he admits therefore only isolated individuals, without relationships between them, he denies the εἴδη [forms, or ideas] of Socrates and Plato, and he limits himself to nominalism.

These same opinions were also adopted by his disciple Menedemus of Eretria, who, of this principle that two different things are not the same, concludes that the good differs from the useful; he rejects all negative propositions and all those that are not simple among the affirmatives, under the pretext that any other proposition is a complex assemblage of terms which do not have any relationship among them.

Thus, Antisthenes' logic, abandoned by his disciples, does not find representatives except in the school of Megara and that of Eretria, and it was bound to disappear with these schools which lost no time falling into complete discredit.

Considered in itself and from the philosophical point of view, this logic does not lack merit. In fact, Antisthenes was right to maintain that opposites cannot co-exist in the same subject and cannot simultaneously be asserted by the mind; by recognizing identity as an essential characteristic of being, by proclaiming the natural rectitude of the intelligence, he sought certitude in the direct and immediate relationship between thought and its object, and he gave to science an unshakeable basis. To be sure, it is an honor for the ancient pupil of the Sophists to have maintained and proven with such force the legitimacy of an important order of our knowledge, I mean to say all our experimental knowledge. Unfortunately, the insistence with which he developed that extremely true opinion and pursued its consequences, led him far afield and far from the truth itself. That intimate union of the mind and reality is undoubtedly a source of perfect certainty, and one cannot see how it would give way to error. But that is not to say, as Antisthenes thought, that it is the only source of our knowledge, that for each thing there is only one idea: that which it directly produces and engraves in the mind; that, on the other hand, each thought corresponds with an object that it is the proper representation of. He was led thus to deny, in an absolute manner, both error and contradiction, and this opinion, which appears at first a strange paradox, is with him the result of his entire faith and the absolute confidence with which he accepts all ideas determined in the mind by reality itself.

One must blame him for not having recognized the role and legitimacy of that natural activity regulated by method, the activity by which the mind arrives at general knowledge and sheds light on rational principles. After having assured himself of a solid basis, I mean to say the idea that the individual object determines in our intelligence, Antisthenes does not attempt to erect the logical edifice of knowledge. If he had like Socrates investigated generalization and accepted definition, he could have established a vast experimental philosophy, just as the Stoics tried to do soon thereafter. Perhaps he thought that by according more to the activity of the mind he would provoke anew and that he would authorize all the temerities, all the excesses of the Physicists, Eleatics, and Sophists: but was it not, through a just fear of error, tantamount to reducing the mind to an insupportable sterility, to proscribing knowledge itself with hypotheses, and the truest and noblest doctrines with false systems, that of Socrates and Plato? One can praise Antisthenes' reserve and prudence, but we must recognize in him a lack of philosophical penetration, something already leveled against him by the best judges among the ancients.

By suppressing general knowledge, he shut himself up in a sort of nominalism. From there, the examination of the true meaning of words, and the in-

vestigation of expression assumed an extreme importance in his eyes; one can hand it to him for having
presented several exceptionally just views on this
subject, for having applied himself to grammatical
studies and for having contributed to giving them a
place of honor. But the interest that can be had by
considering this first attempt at nominalism in antiquity, the originality of Antisthenes' theory, and the
promising developments that it may have led him to,
cannot allow us to forget how far such a system is
from the truth.

That logic of Antisthenes which denies rational knowledge and general ideas, which suppresses
all definition, which rejects contradiction and error, is
consequently essentially critical and negative: it reveals a natural disposition in him that dominates both
in his physics and in his ethics. Xenophon defined the
genius of the Cynic philosopher well when he said
that he is primarily able to combat and to refute, μάλα
ἐλεγκτικός, and, as it turns out, the name itself of *Antisthenes* admirably expresses the two characteristic
traits of his mind, fighting and force (ἀντὶ σθένος).

We now arrive at Antisthenes' ethics, and we investigate, from a historical perspective, both what its origin has been and what its influence.

Antisthenes is not, like Plato, nor Aristotle,
one of those minds that possesses a profound knowledge of the earlier systems of philosophy; he did not
study, or compare, the opinions of others, to borrow
from them what truths they had; he understood in his

own way the teachings of Socrates and he was faithful to himself; doubtless one could find curious analogies between his morality and that of Pythagoras, that of Democritus; but such comparisons would have something of the artificial about them and little usefulness; because the direct influence of Socrates dominated and effaced all others: it is in his doctrine that one must seek out the primary source of Antisthenes' ethics.

Let us recall that Socrates, who finds fault with vain speculations and who wants that every science should have a practical and moral goal; that Socrates who turns all thoughts toward the active life and defines justice through his actions; that Socrates who, by a continuous effort over himself, inured himself to every fatigue, overcame all his passions, made himself superior to events, – that is the master whom Antisthenes admires and imitates.

But this virtue that Socrates teaches is more enlightened, it is more measured and more humane than that of the Cynics.

It is through the spirit of observation and moral analysis that Socrates was primarily a great reformer: as for the study of oneself as the point of departure of every science and every virtue, he spends his life examining himself and interrogating others; thanks to this perfect understanding of man, he excels at guiding his fellow men in the investigation of the true, the beautiful, and the good. He did not create a logic; but he founded a method that he teaches by his example; and one recognizes in his able dialectic, in his investigation of definitions and general truths, the master of Plato. He left the universal science of nature to the side, but he contemplated and admired order and harmony in the world, lifted his thought up to God whom he recognized the existence and perfections of; he finds in God the very origin of justice and virtue, and he shows himself to be full of faith in his Providence.

That divine inspiration, that daemon, that genius of Socrates, is no longer felt in Antisthenes. He finds fault, often for the pleasure of finding fault, and his disciples are more and more animated by that critical and aggressive mind; they strive less to develop in others a love for the good, than to interest them in, and astonish them by, their lively repartees, by their mordant ridicule. Antisthenes says little about self-observation or self-interrogation; he regards reflection as a secondary condition of wisdom; and his successors claim to arrive at virtue without the assistance of the intellect. His ethics seems to have been formed all on its own; independent, like the wise man, it remains isolated, without connection to his logic or physics; and Diogenes will definitively reject these two sciences which he considers unhelpful and even harmful. Socrates had gone so far as to identify wisdom with knowledge of the good, virtue with science: the Cynic school, after having put wisdom and virtue into action alone, finishes by confusing them with external practices and loses itself in a ridiculous formalism.

Socrates taught people to moderate their desires, to master their passions; but he never thought that people needed to kill and destroy every sensibility. Thus, he attaches man to family affections, and, if he prefers not to take part in public affairs, if he finds fault with the errors and excesses of democracy, he is full of submission and respect for the laws, full of love for and devotion to his fatherland.

What distinguishes the Cynic school is its war declared on sensual nature. Antisthenes leaves only friendship in the heart of man; he respects neither feelings of pudor, nor affections for the family, nor love for the fatherland, nor submission to its laws; and, if he has still maintained some restraint, the temerarious ardor of his successors shows none. Under the pretext of arriving at insensibility and testifying to their independence, they defy everything that men venerate, and, thinking to elevate themselves above the vulgar or the common, they do away with all human feelings.

Thus, Socrates' philosophy presents the germ of the Cynics' ethics; but, more intelligent and more reflective, inspired by true science, it has more dignity and nobility in it; ever moderated, it establishes in the soul a perfect subordination and happy harmony under the empire of reason.

Why then did Antisthenes distance himself from Socrates' doctrine? It is what one will understand when one takes full stock of the circumstances around which his philosophy was formed and developed.

He sought to react against the Sophists, his first teachers, and against Aristippus, his co-disciple.

The Sophists presented virtue as easy; it was,

they said, a science, and they taught that science at a particular price. Antisthenes puts wisdom in behavior, virtue in actions, and makes exercise, work, and toil the condition of the good. The more the Sophists debased man, the more the Cynics sought to reinvigorate his moral forces, to raise his character, and to reestablish his dignity.

On the other hand, while the school of the Cyrenaics conflates the good with pleasure, Antisthenes identifies it with virtue, and virtue with effort and toil.

So two rival philosophies, having emerged from the Socratic school, represented two conditions of perfect happiness: on the one side, a predilection for well-being, the satisfaction of all our tendencies, the use of all our goods; on the other, work, virtue, self-control, perfect independence. For the instruction of the subsequent ages and for the progress of philosophy, what was needed was that these two great faces of the question of sovereign good should be strongly exposed to the light, by two schools whose vigorous opposition made them look both exaggerated and exclusive. If Antisthenes hadn't been led on by that fight against Aristippus, would he have ever gone so far as to say that pleasure is an ill, that toil is a good, that absolute independence is man's goal?

The Sophists' philosophy and that of the Cyrenaics was none other than the highest expression of the state of mind and state of ethics [at that time]; hence, their success and their unfortunate influence. The Greek people, in contact with the nations that it had conquered or that commerce had put them into contact with, had witnessed a degeneration of their ancient customs and mores. Wealth was accrued and with it luxury, softness, corruption; while rapid progress was made in the letters and in the arts, simplicity and the male virtue of the first ages had disappeared. The time had come for a vigorous protest to manifest itself, and the reaction was all the more natural in Athens where certain minds never stopped dreaming of Sparta. If Socrates, strongly attached to his fatherland, had never given an example of those poorly reflected sympathies for Athens' rival, there would clearly never have been a philosopher of the Cynosarges. His moral system presented remarkable parallels with the institutions of Lycurgus and the customs of Sparta; and the admiration that they inspired in Diogenes led this latter to profoundly modify and exaggerate the doctrine of his teacher [Antisthenes].

Finally, the spirit of the Cynic school is attached to a more direct and intimate cause, to the social condition in which its representatives found themselves and to the particular nature of their characters.

It must not be forgotten that this school was founded by a νόθος, that it developed at the [gymnasium of the] Cynosarges and recruited disciples from among outcasts and slaves, except for later making several adepts and proselytes from among the more elevated ranks, except for converting and fanaticizing one Crates. From within these scorned and suffering classes emerged beautiful thoughts on the work that they sought to rehabilitate, on virtue and true dignity, on absolute independence and perfect liberty, on the equality of men who were all considered as members of the same city-state.

Antisthenes, Diogenes, Crates stood out by a great energy, by an astonishing austerity: their philosophy, it is their behavior and, I would say, the tension of their soul. Hence, whatever there is of the excessive in that morality which, instead of taking men such as they are and thinking about what they can do or become, demands even more rare qualities [from them] and proposes only extraordinary struggles and violent remedies.

Such is the ethical philosophy of the Cynics in summary; it is a great Socratic idea, collected and exaggerated by poor and harsh men who position it in strong opposition to the influence of the Sophists and Cyrenaics, and who strive, by the vehemence of their criticisms and the rigor of their principles, to stop the advance of luxury and the corruption of mores.

If Diogenes, Crates, and their successors made the Cynic school fall rapidly into complete discredit, Antisthenes' doctrine had however, through its influence on other schools, a powerful effect on the destinies of philosophy.

To begin with, Stilpon, a disciple of Diogenes, attempts to regenerate the school of Megara by accepting and tempering the moral principles of the Cynics, whose doctrine and life recall αὐτάρκεια and ἀπάθεια. Forgetting his teacher's exaggerations in order to collect all his noble and generous ideas, he shows what the Cynic philosophy can actually become when it encounters great characters with upright and cultivated minds.

But why stop at these secondary similarities? Is it not enough for the glory of Antisthenes to have prepared the way for Stoicism which is merely a vast and scientific development of his ethical philosophy?

Zeno of Citium is a disciple of Stilpon and Crates; this latter [philosopher] directly introduced him to the Cynic philosophy and had the most decisive influence on his mind. Also, Zeno and his successors mention Antisthenes, Diogenes, and Crates with praise and admiration, and they regard Cynic philosophy as a shortcut for arriving at virtue, σύντομος ἐπ᾽ ἀρετὴν ὁδός. The ancients often noticed the similarities that unite these two schools; they have always linked Stoicism to Cynicism from the beginning, and they regarded Antisthenes as the first author of that great philosophical movement.

Zeno separated from Diogenes and Crates by bringing his mind to bear on the sciences that they had scorned; he elevated himself above Antisthenes by embracing philosophical questions in the unity of a vast system.

But one would be remiss not to point out that the general idea that dominates all his philosophy and ties the different parts of it together is the very idea that formed the basis of Cynic ethics, the idea of a force that exerts itself, of a cause that struggles and develops. The general principle of the Stoics' physics is the tension of the universal force existing everywhere in matter; for them, the criterium of sensation, the source of comprehension and of knowledge, is the tension of the soul, and that same tension is the indispensable condition of virtue; according to Cleanthes, it is virtue itself.

Their ethics is, like that of the Cynics, the ethics of effort, and, in fact, they also consider life as a struggle between two irreconcilable principles, freedom and passion, and they bring together all the forces of the soul for this internal combat which must destroy not only base desires but the noblest and most generous tendencies.

Virtue, they say, is the unique purpose of life; it is the sovereign good: but they are not content with showing, along with Antisthenes, that the wise man no longer has anything to desire, that he possesses the true goods, the riches of the soul: they go further and say that he brings all the goods together. On the other hand, regarding as equally bad all the actions that are contrary to the absolute good, they assert that all faults are equal. Finally, they recognize that this proud virtue is above human strength. Diogenes said that it was difficult to find a man really worthy of the name; the Stoics avow that the wise man has never existed and think that he never will exist.

That said, they have generally avoided the excesses of the new Cynics and imitated the reserve and moderation of Antisthenes. Thus, they have not at all gone as far as those voluntary rigors, as far as those imposed privations, as far as that type of asceticism that the Diogenes and the Crates [of the world] have given the example of. They have very poorly controlled the appetites of man, but they did not authorize him to defy any decency or to turn his shamelessness into a glory.

Their ethics is not a new and original doctrine; all the great principles on which it rests, all the fecund ideas, all the proud maxims, are already found in Antisthenes and Diogenes. But what makes the ethics of the Stoics superior to that of the Cynic school is that they have recognized the necessity to cultivate and clarify the intelligence in order to regulate behavior, and they regarded self-reflection and instruction as indispensable to arriving at virtue and realizing the good. That is why their ethics is a systematic and rigorous ensemble of clearly-formulated principles and capably-deduced consequences; they closely associate it with the other parts of their philosophy, and methodically explain it with exact definitions and numerous divisions which emphasize a precision of ideas and a certain depth in psychological analysis.

From within the school of Zeno a protestation arose in favor of the simplest and coarsest doctrine of Diogenes and Crates: Aristo of Chios left Portugal and went to teach at the Gymnasium that Antisthenes had made famous. He rejected all sciences, even logic and physics, and after having reduced philosophy to ethics, he removed from it the scientific character that Zeno had given to it.

This attempt by Aristo did not have lasting results; it was left for the Stoics to represent the great principles developed with originality by Antisthenes, accepted with so much ardor by Diogenes; they had the merit of elevating the Cynic doctrine to the rank of a science and putting it in harmony with the state of philosophy and the needs of the mind; and, thus transformed by them, it spread out like a consolation and a support until the last days of paganism and ancient civilization. If the founder of the Cynic school had not had, on the beliefs and destinies of humanity, so general and so definitive an influence as Plato did, it needs to be recognized that in the Greek and Roman worlds his action was more immediate and tangible.

What is the philosophic value of Antisthenes' ethics?

It does not attach itself, like that of Socrates, to a religious doctrine, and it does not rest on the superior authority of reason illuminated by God himself. It is within man, and within him alone, that it claims to find the beginning and end of our activity. For this reason, it is unable to establish, among the diverse faculties of the soul, a just equilibrium and a harmonious concours. The more or less avowed pretension of the Cynic school is to realize the good without the help of intelligence, by the destruction of sensibility, and by the sole effort of the will.

But what is ethics without knowledge? What is wisdom without reflection? To pretend that one has arrived at virtue and that one owes nothing to intelligence, – is it not a strange ignorance of one's self and a bizarre inconsequence? Our actions owe all their value to thought itself; and this activity in which the new Cynics make virtue consist is nothing more than a poorly reflected and blind activity; they scorned Socrates' cultivated reason and admired only his strength of soul; and as they rejected one of the essential elements of moral perfection, nothing directs their efforts, nothing tempers their energy, and their vain wisdom loses itself in the extravagance of an entirely external practice.

They clearly showed the danger of the passions, the necessity of freeing oneself from their servitude, the usefulness of work and toil in order to perfect ourselves and to make ourselves better; but they did not see that true morality must develop our nature all the while regulating it, and not by destroying a part of it, to guide man and not mutilate him. They waged a pointless battle against themselves and they consumed themselves in vain efforts in order to arrive at that sublime impassibility, at that ideal insensibility.

What remains, finally, is the will whose predominant and excessive development is the very foundation of Cynic philosophy. The exercise of the will, in other words, effort and tension, is, it is true, an indispensable condition of virtue; but it is not the only condition: the will itself has need of being illuminated by the intelligence, of being excited and supported by all the noble and generous tendencies. To seek in it the rule of our conduct, that is to go astray and, in reality, to suppress all moral law; simultaneously as that freedom and independence so vaunted by the Cynics frees the wise man from the seductions of pleasure and the attachment to external goods, they teach him to reflect on himself like the only judge of the merit of his actions, to scorn customs and usages, institutions and laws, and to defy the most respectable sentiments and most sacred duties.

Such is the Cynic philosophy, a surprising combination of great moral truths and unfortunate exaggerations. When it considered virtue as absolute insensibility and perfect independence, and that superhuman virtue as the unique goal in life, it went astray in a chimerical and impotent attempt. Consequently, it will find only a small number of adepts; but those who become attached to it will do so with that passion and fanaticism that a doctrine always inspires, for which one must sacrifice much and suffer much.

Other Books by the Publisher

Fanchette's Pretty Little Foot by Restif de la Bretonne

Je M'Accuse... by Léon Bloy

My Hospitals & My Prisons by Paul Verlaine

Salvation Through the Jews by Léon Bloy

Words of a Demolitions Contractor by Léon Bloy

Cellulely by Paul Verlaine

Ecclesiastical Laurels by Jacques Rochette de la Morlière

Flowers of Bitumen by Émile Goudeau

Songs for Her & Odes in Her Honor by Paul Verlaine

On Huysmans' Tomb by Léon Bloy

Ten Years a Bohemian by Émile Goudeau

The Soul of Napoleon by Léon Bloy

Blood of the Poor by Léon Bloy

Joan of Arc and Germany by Léon Bloy

A Platonic Love by Paul Alexis

The Revealer of the Globe: Christopher Columbus & His Future Beatification (Part One) by Léon Bloy

An Immodest Proposal by Dr. Helmut Schleppend

The Pornographer by Restif de la Bretonne

Style (Theory and History) by Ernest Hello

www.ingramcontent.com/pod-product-compliance
Lightning Source LLC
Chambersburg PA
CBHW031528120626
46545CB00005B/2054